IN THE HANDS
OF A BAKER

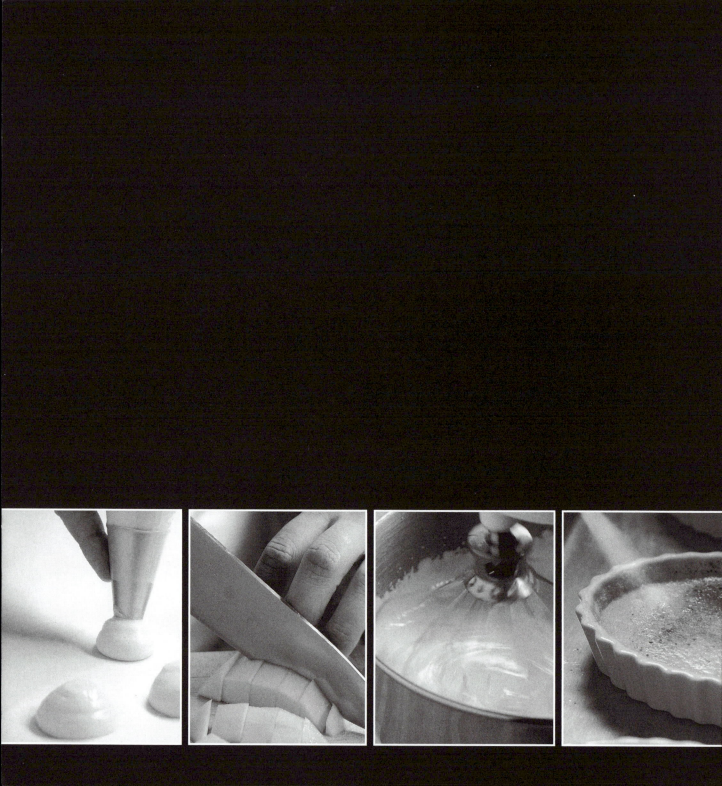

IN THE HANDS
OF A BAKER

The Culinary Institute of America

PHOTOGRAPHY BY BEN FINK

WILEY

THE CULINARY INSTITUTE OF AMERICA

President	Dr. Tim Ryan '77, CMC, AAC
Provost	Mark Erickson '77, CMC
Director of Publishing	Nathalie Fischer
Editorial Project Manager	Margaret Wheeler '00
Editorial Assistants	Erin Jeanne McDowell '08
	Laura Monroe '12

Published by John Wiley & Sons, Inc., Hoboken, New Jersey

Published simultaneously in Canada

Library of Congress Cataloging-in-Publication Data:
In the hands of a baker / The Culinary Institute of America ; photography by Ben Fink.
    p. cm.
  Includes index.
  ISBN 978-0-470-58785-0 (pbk.)
1. Baking. 2. Baked products industry. 3. Baking—Vocational guidance. I. Culinary Institute of America.
  TX763.I46 2013
  641.81'5--dc23
                            2011045253

Printed in the United States of America

10 9 8 7 6 5 4 3 2 1

CONTENTS

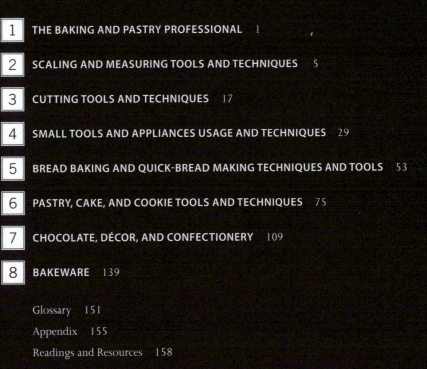

ACKNOWLEDGMENTS

The Culinary Institute of America wishes to recognize the contributions of the following individuals for their work on this book:

Ben Fink for the beautiful photography.

We are grateful to all those who helped on the photo shoots for this book but we could not have accomplished them without the invaluable help of Robert Kristof and Lauren Fury. We would also not have had all of the equipment necessary were it not for Chef Peter Greweling and Chef Kate Cavotti.

Finally, a big thank you to Warren Kitchen & Cutlery in Rhinebeck, New York. Richard von Husen and James Zitz, co-owners of the store, graciously provided many of the tools featured in the book.

INTRODUCTION

All great craftsmen and artists rely on their tools. Finding the right tool for the task is a more complex activity than simply picking up the nearest paint brush or chisel and beginning to work. The way the tool is made, the way it fits in the hand, the materials used in its construction, and the purpose for which it is intended all play a part in producing the best possible tool for an individual chef.

Today's bakers and pastry chefs have a wide array of tools available to them. A basic selection of tools, a knife kit, is indispensable but it may need to be expanded depending on the work that needs to be accomplished. There are specific tools that the professional needs in order to produce the highest-quality cakes, cookies, pastries, and breads. There are even more specialized tools that are needed for creating chocolates and confections and many types of décor. The investment in these tools can be substantial but it is worth it in order to increase the amount of work that the professional can produce in his or her repertoire.

The novice baker will find information about, and skills and procedures for, using an assortment of baking and pastry tools properly and safely in the kitchen. Professional bakers and pastry chefs charged with training their staff will find this a useful, thorough training tool, progressing from the basic scaling and measuring tools, to small tools and appliances, and finally to specialized tools for bread baking, chocolates and confections, and décor. It is vital for professionals to continue educating themselves about the tools that are frequently being updated and improved and those new technologies that will help to make their jobs easier and create beautiful products more easily.

For those of you using this book in a classroom or training setting, a password-protected Wiley Instructor Book Companion website devoted entirely to this book (www.wiley.com/college/cia) provides access to **PowerPoint** lecture slides and additional website resources.

1

THE BAKING AND PASTRY PROFESSIONAL

As important as physical tools are for the professional baker and pastry chef, knowledge of the industry is just as vital and can be used in a similar fashion—as a tool to further a career. Just as formal education has become important in launching a career, certification and continuing education keep advancing you as a baking arts professional. Because the industry is constantly evolving, continuing your education by attending workshops, seminars, and trade shows hones your skills while allowing you to keep up with new methods, ingredients, techniques, products, and business skills.

Throughout your career, you should evaluate your achievements and goals; take the appropriate steps to keep on top of the latest information geared to both culinary professionals and the world at large; enter contests and competitions; and educate yourself by learning to use the important tools of your business, from the latest technology or software to the latest pastry tool.

CAREER OPPORTUNITIES FOR BAKING AND PASTRY PROFESSIONALS

Bakers and pastry chefs can pursue many options. You might own your own company or work for someone else. It could be a commissary setting, restaurant, or shop specializing in wedding cakes or handcrafted breads. Bakers often follow one of two paths, working in large commercial bakeries that do volume production or smaller shops that produce less volume but higher-quality goods. To get a foundation you might work in a cross section of bakeries and kitchens and then specialize in a discipline.

Wholesale bakeshops focus on large-scale production, selling finished or unbaked items and batters to supermarkets, cafés, gourmet shops, restaurants, caterers, cafeterias, and the like. Individually owned shops provide a range of services, from full-service bakeshops to ones that specialize in chocolates and confections or wedding cakes. Large hotels rely upon the skills of pastry chefs and bakers who are often responsible for breakfast pastries, elaborate pastry displays, wedding cakes, and the like, including items for the hotel's many food outlets and banquet rooms.

Restaurants rely on pastry chefs who provide a range of baking and pastry skills to create a variety of items such as ice cream and cakes, chocolates to serve as *mignardises* and petits fours, even pizza dough. Private clubs and executive dining rooms as well as schools, hospitals, and colleges rely upon executive pastry chefs and master bakers to handle high-volume, high-quality fare.

Food producers operate research and development kitchens and hire bakers and pastry chefs to test products and formulas and fine-tune them. These large businesses also offer benefits and career advancement within the corporation.

Pastry chefs and bakers are often hired by caterers to meet the desires of a special client for a particular event, whether a trade convention, wedding, birthday party, cocktail reception, or gallery opening. Grocery stores hire baking and pastry professionals to develop carryout desserts and signature breads, as well as assisting with research, focus groups, packaging, pricing, and marketing strategies. Consultants in the baking and pastry arts work with corporate and restaurant clients to develop menus, staffing strategies, marketing plans, packaging, and the like.

THE BUSINESS OF BAKING AND PASTRY

As your career evolves, you will move into positions where your skills as an executive, administrator, and manager are in demand. This does not mean that your ability to make breads and pastries is less important. Plating, presentation, and pricing are daily concerns for any executive pastry chef or baker—and you may still be creating new menu items and products while keeping costs under control and improving profits. Managing a bakery or pastry shop requires the ability to handle four areas effectively: physical assets, information, people (human resources), and time. The greater your management skills in these areas, the greater your potential for success. Many management systems today emphasize the use of "excellence" as a yardstick. Every area of your operation can be used to improve the quality of service you provide to your customers.

Managing Physical Assets

Physical assets are the equipment and supplies needed to do business: everything from industrial-size mixers to flour to cash registers. In short, anything that affects your ability to do business well. These require control systems that will keep your organization operating at maximum efficiency.

For any baking and pastry operation, the material costs—whatever you use to create, present, sell, and serve your goods—is the biggest expense. For this reason, being a baking and pastry professional entails being your own purchasing agent—or knowing how to work with one—to maintain inventories to produce and market your products and services.

Managing Information

Given the sheer volume of information generated each day, the ability to tap into the information resources you need has never been more important. You must not only keep yourself informed of the latest trends but also develop the ability to look beyond what is current to predict future trends. This will help to keep your business thriving. Restaurants, menus, dining room design, and more change dramatically with societal trends, on-the-go lifestyles, and the interest in world cuisines. Current tastes affect what people eat and where and how they want to eat it. The Internet is a powerful influence as well.

Managing Human Resources

Every shop relies on the work and dedication of people, whether they are the executive pastry chef, the bakers, or waitstaff—to name a few. No matter how large or small your staff may be, a team effort is one of the major factors in your success. One of the hallmarks of the true professional is being a team member—and this team can simply be you, your clients, and suppliers. Being part of a team requires as much practice and concentration as any baking or pastry technique. The best teams are made of talented individuals who bring not only technical skills to the mix but passion for excellence. You can immediately recognize a strong team approach in a successful

bakeshop or pastry kitchen. Everyone knows what work must be done beyond just their job description.

The management of human resources entails legal responsibilities. Everyone has the right to work in an environment that is free from physical hazards and with properly maintained equipment. Liability insurance must be kept up to date and adequate. Taxes on earnings have to be paid to federal, state, and local agencies. Employment packages have to be managed, including life insurance, medical insurance, assistance with dependent care, and even adult literacy training and substance abuse programs. Benefits can make a difference in the caliber of employees you work with or manage.

Managing Time

Learning new skills so that you can make the best possible use of time should be an ongoing part of your career. If you look at your operation carefully, you will discover how time is wasted. In most, the top five time wasters are: lack of clear priorities for tasks, poor staff training, poor communication, poor organization, and inadequate or nonexistent tools for accomplishing tasks. Invest time in these strategies:

▶ *Until you are clear about what needs to be done and in what order, you cannot begin the process of saving time. Consider the way you, your coworkers, and your staff spend the day. Does everyone have a basic understanding of which tasks are most important? Do they know when to begin a particular task in order to finish it on time? It can be an eye-opening experience to take a hard look at where everyone's workday goes.*

▶ **TRAIN OTHERS.** *If you expect someone to do a job properly, take enough time to explain the task carefully. Walk yourself and your staff through the jobs that must be done, and be sure that everyone understands how to do the work, where to find needed* *items, how far individual responsibility extends, and what to do in case a question—or an emergency— comes up. Give your staff the yardsticks they need to evaluate their time and jobs, otherwise you may find yourself squandering precious hours picking up the slack.*

▶ **LEARN TO COMMUNICATE CLEARLY.** *Whether you are training a new employee, introducing a new menu item, or ordering a piece of equipment, clear communication is essential. Be specific and be brief without leaving out necessary information.*

▶ **CREATE AN ORDERLY WORK ENVIRONMENT.** *If you have to dig through five shelves to find the lid to a storage container for buttercream, you are not using your time wisely. Organize work areas carefully, so that tools, ingredients, and equipment are readily available. Schedule—and write out—similar activities so they are performed at the same time and in the same way by different people.*

▶ **PURCHASE, REPLACE, AND MAINTAIN ALL TOOLS AS NECESSARY.** *A well-equipped kitchen has all the tools necessary to prepare every item on the menu. If you are missing something as basic as a sieve, your crème anglaise will not be perfectly smooth. Learn to operate equipment safely and teach others to do the same.*

THE PROFESSION

A professional makes a living from the practice of a craft. Rather than viewing work as simply a means to an end, true professionals have a passion for their craft and a drive for excellence. Some professionals may tell you that they baked for their families or worked in a bakeshop when they were young. Others come to the baking and pastry field after establishing themselves in other areas in the food-service

industry. Still others make a switch to the baking and pastry profession as a second or third career.

All professionals must learn the foundations of the profession—handling ingredients and equipment, and standard or basic formulas. At the next level, they apply those foundations, adapting and modifying formulas or finding ways to improve quality and efficiency in their own work. At the highest level, they draw on all they know and use their knowledge, skills, and creativity to produce something—as specific as a new pastry or as intangible as a successful career—that was not there before.

Every member of a profession is responsible for its image. Those who have made the greatest impression know that the cardinal virtues of the baking and pastry profession are an open and inquiring mind, an appreciation of and dedication to quality and service, and a sense of responsibility—qualities that are cultivated throughout a career.

▶ **COMMITMENT TO SERVICE.** *The food-service industry is predicated on service, and professionals must never lose sight of that. Good service includes (but is not limited to) providing quality items that are properly and safely prepared, appropriately flavored, and attractively presented—in short, what makes the customer happy.*

▶ **RESPONSIBILITY.** *A professional's responsibility is fourfold: to him- or herself, to coworkers, to the business, and to the customer. Waste, disregard for others, and misuse of any commodity are unacceptable. Abusive language and profanity, harassment, and insensitivity to gender, sexuality, and race do not have a place in the professional bakeshop and pastry kitchen. Self-esteem and attitude toward the establishment need to be positive.*

▶ **GOOD JUDGMENT.** *Although not easy to learn, good judgment is a prerequisite for a professional. Good judgment is never completely mastered; rather, it is a goal toward which one can continually strive.*

2

SCALING AND MEASURING TOOLS AND TECHNIQUES

Tools for measuring and portioning are basics in any professional kitchen. Adhering to a recipe's measurements will enable you to accurately order foods so that you have an appropriate inventory of goods on hand, allow you to yield the correct amount of product, and ensure that your portions and servings are consistent in flavor, texture, appearance, and size.

MEASURING WITH PRECISION

Ingredients are purchased and used following one of three measuring conventions: count, volume, or weight. They may be purchased according to one system but measured in another for use in a formula.

Measuring by Count

Count is a measurement of whole items. The terms *each, bunch,* and *dozen* all indicate units of count measure. If an individual item has been processed, graded, or packaged according to established standards, count can be a useful, accurate way to measure that ingredient. It is less accurate for ingredients requiring some preparation before they are added to the formula or for those without any established standards for purchasing. Apples illustrate the point well. If a formula calls for ten apples, then the yield, flavor, and consistency of the finished product will change depending upon whether the apples you use are large or small.

Measuring by Volume

Volume is a measurement of the space occupied by a solid, liquid, or gas. The terms *teaspoon* (tsp), *tablespoon* (tbsp), *fluid ounce* (fl oz), *cup* (c), *pint* (pt), *quart* (qt), *gallon* (gal), *milliliter* (mL), and *liter* (L) all indicate units of volume measure. Graduated containers, measuring cups, and utensils with a precise volume (such as a 2-fluid-ounce/60 mL ladle or a teaspoon) are used to measure volume. Volume measurements are best suited to liquids, though they are also used for dry ingredients, such as spices, that are used in small amounts. Keep in mind that tools used for measuring volume are not always as precise as

they should be. The density of the ingredient being measured can make a big difference with volume measuring tools. A cup of sifted weighs less than a cup of unsifted flour; a cup of packed brown sugar weighs more than a cup of unpacked brown sugar. Also, volume measuring tools need not conform to any regulated standards, so the amount of an ingredient measured with one set of spoons, cups, or pitchers could be quite different from the amount measured with another set.

Measuring by Weight

Weight is a measurement of the mass, or heaviness, of a solid, liquid, or gas. The terms *ounce* (oz), *pound* (lb), *gram* (g), and *kilogram* (kg) all indicate units of weight measure. Scales are used to measure weight, and they must meet specific standards for accuracy regulated by the U.S. National Institute of Standards and Technology's Office of Weights and Measures. In professional kitchens, weight is usually the preferred type of measurement because it is easier to be accurate with weight than with volume measurements.

SCALES

Scales must be used correctly to be effective. You want the weight of only the ingredient, not the ingredient and the container holding it. Before using any scale, you must take certain steps to account for the weight of the container. This process is known as *setting a scale to tare* or *setting a scale to zero.*

Beam Balance Scale

A beam balance (or baker's) scale has two platforms attached on either end of a beam. The point where

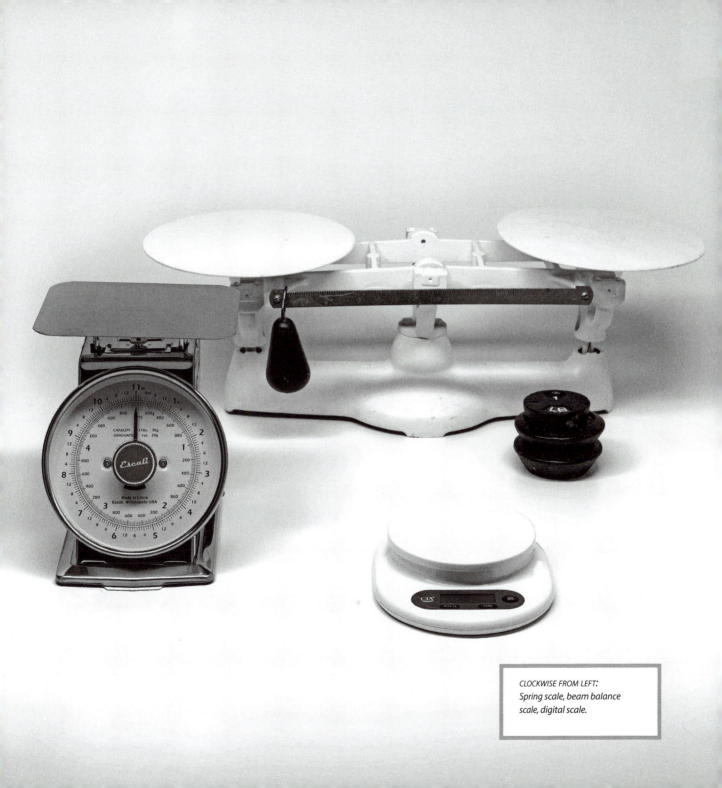

CLOCKWISE FROM LEFT:
Spring scale, beam balance scale, digital scale.

the beam and the base meet is the fulcrum. At the front of the scale, a weight hangs from a bar notched at 1-oz/28-g increments. To tare, set the container on the scale and reset the scale so that both sides are level, either by manipulating the weight on the front of the scale or by adding a counterweight to the other side of the scale. To weigh out an ingredient, slide the hanging weight to the correct notch. To find an ingredient's weight, move the hanging weight until the platforms are level. To set the scale to zero, make sure that the two platforms are level. Beam balances can measure quantities far greater than the maximum weight shown on the scale if counterweights (typically available in 1-, 2-, and 4-lb/454-g, 907-g, and 1.81-kg weights) are used. To use a counterweight, set the counterweight on the right platform. Then add enough of the given ingredient to the left platform to make the two platforms level.

Spring Scale

A spring scale has a platform set on top of a pedestal that contains a spring mechanism for weighing and a dial indicator on the front. To tare a spring scale, place the container for measuring the ingredients on the scale and turn the dial so that the pointer or arrow is aligned with zero. Spring scales are designed to read in any number of increments. Some are very sensitive and can measure small amounts, while others are made so that they only measure in large increments.

Digital Scale

A digital scale has a stainless-steel platform set on an electronic base with a digital display. Scales capable of measuring very small amounts typically have a smaller total capacity. Scales capable of weighing large amounts (more than 4 lb/1.81 kg) are less sensitive when measuring small amounts. To tare a digital scale, you press a button to reset the scale to zero. Most digital scales can switch between metric and U.S. standard weight systems.

VOLUME MEASURING TOOLS

Graduated pitchers or beakers and measuring cups and spoons are commonly used in the bakeshop to measure liquids and pourable ingredients (eggs, molasses, or corn syrup, for example). Pitchers and cups are scaled off with lines or markings to show varying measures. Clear pitchers and cups are easy to fill accurately. For the most accurate results, use the smallest measure possible to measure ingredients, place the vessel on a level surface, and bend down to take the reading at eye level.

Dry measuring cups are commonly used in recipes written for the home baker. In the bakeshop, they are used to measure small amounts of certain dry ingredients, such as salt, spices, and baking soda. To use measuring cups and spoons for dry ingredients, overfill the measure, then use a straightedge to scrape the excess away; the ingredient should fill the measure evenly up to the rim.

BAKING FORMULAS

Always read through any formula completely before you start. The formula may require a special piece of equipment or a component made separately. Or perhaps the formula makes only ten servings and you

CLOCKWISE FROM BOTTOM RIGHT: Measuring spoons, measuring cups, plastic liquid measuring cup, metal liquid measuring pitcher.

need to make fifty. In that case, you will have to scale the formula. In increasing or decreasing a formula, you may discover that you need to make equipment modifications as well. Once you have read through and evaluated or modified the formula, assemble your equipment and ingredients—the baker's *mise en place*. In many formulas, the ingredients list will indicate how the ingredient should be prepared (for example, sifted, melted, or cut into pieces of a certain size) before the actual mixing or assembling begins.

Standardized Formulas

The formulas used in a professional baking and pastry setting must be standardized. Unlike published formulas meant to work in a variety of settings for a wide audience, standardized formulas suit the specific needs of an individual pastry kitchen or bakeshop. Preparing well-written and accurate standardized formulas is a big part of the professional pastry chef's or baker's work, as these are records that include much more than just ingredient names and preparation steps. Standardized formulas establish overall yields, serving sizes, holding and serving practices, and plating information. They also set standards for equipment as well as temperatures and times for cooking or baking. These standards help to ensure consistent quality and quantity, and they permit pastry chefs and bakers to gauge the efficiency of their work and reduce costs by eliminating waste as appropriate.

Standardized formulas can be handwritten or stored on a computer, using a formula management program or other such database or program. As you prepare a standardized formula, be as precise and consistent as possible. Include as many of the following elements as necessary:

▶ **NAME OR TITLE** *of the food item or dish.*

▶ **YIELD FOR THE FORMULA,** *expressed as one or more of the following: total weight, total volume, or total number of servings.*

▶ **PORTION INFORMATION FOR EACH SERVING,** *expressed as one or more of the following: number of items (count), volume, or weight.*

▶ **INGREDIENT NAMES,** *expressed in appropriate detail (specifying variety or brand as necessary).*

▶ **INGREDIENT MEASURES,** *expressed as one or more of the following: count, volume, or weight.*

▶ **INGREDIENT PREPARATION INSTRUCTIONS,** *sometimes included in the ingredient name, sometimes included in the method as a separate step.*

▶ **EQUIPMENT INFORMATION** *for preparation, cooking, storing, holding, and serving.*

▶ **PREPARATION STEPS** *detailing mise en place, mixing, cooking or baking, and temperatures for safe food handling.*

▶ **SERVICE INFORMATION,** *including how to finish and plate the dessert; sauces and garnishes, if any; and proper service temperatures.*

▶ **HOLDING AND REHEATING PROCEDURES,** *including equipment, times, temperatures, and safe storage.*

▶ **CRITICAL CONTROL POINTS (CCPS)** *at appropriate stages in the formula, to indicate temperatures and times for safe food-handling procedures during storage, preparation, holding, and reheating.*

Formula Calculations

Often you will need to modify a formula. Sometimes the yield must be increased or decreased. You may be adapting a formula from another source to a standardized format, or you may be adjusting a standardized formula for a special event, such as a banquet or a reception. You may need to convert from volume measures to weight, or from metric measurements to the U.S. system, or you may want to determine how much the ingredients in a particular formula cost.

The Formula Conversion Factor (FCF)

To increase or decrease the yield of a formula, you need to determine the formula conversion factor. Once you know that factor, you then multiply all the ingredient amounts by it and convert the new measurements into appropriate formula units for your pastry kitchen or bakeshop. This may require converting items listed by count into weight or volume measurements, or rounding measurements to reasonable quantities. And in some cases you will have to make a judgment call about those ingredients that do not scale up or down exactly, such as spices, salt, thickeners, and leaveners.

> Formula conversion factor (FCF) = Desired yield/Original yield

The desired yield and the original yield must be expressed in the same way before you can use the formula; that is, both must be in the same unit of measure. For example, if the original formula gives the yield in ounces and you want to make 2 quarts of the sauce, you will need to convert quarts into fluid ounces. And, if your original formula says that it makes five servings and does not list the size of each serving, you may need to test the formula to determine serving size.

Converting to a Common Unit of Measure

To convert measurements to a common unit (by weight or volume), use the following formulas. This information can be used both to convert scaled measurements into practical and easy-to use formula measures and to determine costs. For some ingredients, straightforward multiplication or division is all that is needed. To increase a formula for poached pears from five servings to fifty, for example, you would simply multiply five pears by ten; no further adjustments are necessary. But once you have converted them, some other ingredient amounts may need some fine-tuning. You may need to round off a result or convert it to the most logical unit of measure. And measures for ingredients such as thickeners, spices, seasonings, and leavenings, for example, should not always be simply multiplied or divided.

Other considerations when converting formula yields include the equipment you have, the production issues you face, and the skill level of your staff. Rewrite steps as necessary to suit the realities of your establishment at this point. It is important to do this now, so you can discover any further changes to the ingredients or methods that the new yield might cause.

Converting for a different number of servings

Sometimes you need to modify the total yield of a formula to obtain a different number of servings.
Number of servings × Serving size = Total yield
For instance, you may have a sauce formula that makes four servings of 2 fl oz/60 mL each, but you

want to make forty servings of 2 fl oz/60 mL each. To make the conversion:

First determine the total original yield of the formula and the total desired yield.

4 × 2 fl oz = 8 fl oz (total original yield)
40 × 2 fl oz = 80 fl oz (total desired yield)

Then determine the formula conversion factor.

$\dfrac{80\ \text{fl oz}}{8\ \text{fl oz}}$ = 10 (the formula conversion factor or FCF)

Modify the formula as described above by multiplying formula measures by 10.

Converting for a different serving size

Sometimes you need to modify the total yield of a formula to obtain a different number of servings of a different size. For instance, you may have a sauce formula that makes four servings of 2 fl oz/60 mL each, but you want to make twenty 3-fl oz/90-mL servings. To make the conversion:

First determine the total original yield of the formula and the total desired yield.

4 × 2 fl oz = 8 fl oz (total original yield)
20 × 3 fl oz = 60 fl oz (total desired yield)

Then determine the formula conversion factor.

$\dfrac{60}{8}$ = 7.5 (the formula conversion factor or FCF)

Modify the formula as described above by multiplying formula measures by 7.5.

VOLUME VERSUS WEIGHT MEASURE

In the professional bakery or pastry shop, most ingredients are measured by weight. When creating standardized formulas for common use, consistency of quality and flavor is the most important objective. Weight is more accurate, leaving less room for error. If a formula is found or developed in volume measurements it should be converted to weight for professional use.

Converting volume measures to weight

Confusion often arises between weight and volume measures when ounces are the unit of measure. It is important to remember that weight is measured in ounces (oz) and volume is measured in fluid ounces (fl oz). A standard volume measuring cup is equal to 8 fl oz, but the contents of the cup may not always weigh 8 oz/227 g. One cup (8 fl oz/240 mL) of shredded fresh coconut weighs just under 3 oz/85 g, but 1 cup (8 fl oz/240 mL) of peanut butter weighs 9 oz/255 g. Since measuring dry ingredients by weight is much more accurate, it is the preferred and most common method used for measuring dry ingredients in professional kitchens and bakeshops.

Water is the only substance for which it can be safely assumed that 1 fl oz/30 mL (a volume measure) equals 1 oz/28 g by weight. But you can convert the volume measure of another ingredient into a weight if you know how much a cup of the ingredient (prepared as required by the formula) weighs. This information is available in a number of charts or ingredients databases. You can also calculate and record the information yourself:

▶ *Record a description of the ingredient and the way it is received (whole, frozen, chopped, canned, etc.).*

- *Prepare the ingredient as directed by the formula (sift flour, roast nuts, chop or melt chocolate, drain items packed in syrup, and so on). Record this advance preparation, too.*

- *Measure the ingredient carefully according to the formula, using nested measures for dry ingredients or liquid cups or pitchers for liquid ingredients.*

- *Set up your scale and set it to tare.*

- *Weigh the ingredient.*

- *Finally, record the weight of the ingredient with the modifier recorded in the proper place.*

Converting Between U.S. and Metric Measurement Systems

The metric system used throughout the rest of the world is a decimal system, meaning that it is based on multiples of ten. The gram is the basic unit of weight, the liter the basic unit of volume, and the meter the basic unit of length. Prefixes added to the basic units indicate larger or smaller units. The U.S. system uses ounces and pounds to measure weight, and teaspoons, tablespoons, fluid ounces, cups, pints, quarts, and gallons to measure volume. Unlike the metric system, the U.S. system is not based on multiples of a particular number, so it is not as simple to increase or decrease quantities. Rather, the equivalencies of the different units of measure must be memorized or derived from a chart. Most modern measuring equipment is capable of measuring in both U.S. and metric units. If, however, a formula is written in a system of measurement for which you do not have the proper measuring equipment, you will need to convert to the other system.

To convert ounces and pounds to metric:

> Multiply ounces by 28.35 to determine grams.
> Divide pounds by 2.2 to determine kilograms.

To convert metric grams to ounces or pounds:

> Divide grams by 28.35 to determine ounces.
> Divide grams by 454 to determine pounds.

To convert fluid ounces to metric milliliters:

> Multiply fluid ounces by 30 to determine milliliters.

To convert metric milliliters to fluid ounces:

> Divide milliliters by 30 to determine fluid ounces.

To convert Celsius to Fahrenheit:

> Multiply the degrees Celsius by 9. Divide the result by 5, and add 32 to get the Fahrenheit equivalent.
> $(°C \times 9) + 32 = °F\ 5$

To convert Fahrenheit to Celsius:

> Subtract 32 from the degrees Fahrenheit. Multiply the result by 5, and divide the result by 9 to get the Celsius equivalent.
> $(°F - 32) \times 5 = °C$

THERMOMETERS

Any bakeshop should have thermometers capable of measuring accurately over a wide range of temperatures. Instant-read thermometers are available with both dial and digital readouts. Digital thermometers typically measure a wider range of temperatures more accurately than dial type thermometers can, and they are usually more accurate when measuring shallow liquids.

Instant-Read Thermometer

Instant-read thermometers are available with both dial and digital readouts. Instant-read thermometers are most useful when working with chocolate, yeast doughs, and other sensitive batters.

Candy Thermometer

Candy (or sugar or deep-fat) thermometers may be calibrated in degrees only; others also indicate the most commonly used stages for sugar cooking (such as thread, soft ball, and hard crack). Candy thermometers should register from 100° to 400°F/38° to 204°C and should be able to withstand temperatures up to 500°F/260°C.

Stem Thermometer

Stem-type thermometers are excellent for checking the internal temperature of products such as doughs or custards; they can also be used to check the temperature of liquids. These thermometers consist of a long stem with a digital or dial head that indicates the temperature.

Probe Thermometer

Probe thermometers consist of a plastic digital-readout base with a metal probe on the end of a cord; some have an alarm setting to indicate that a specific temperature has been reached.

Checking a Thermometer's Accuracy

To check a thermometer's accuracy, let it stand for 10 minutes in boiling water. It should read 212°F/100°C. If there is a discrepancy, subtract or add the correct number of degrees whenever using the thermometer to make up for the difference.

Almond Dragées

MAKES 110 PIECES

INGREDIENT	U.S.	METRIC
Sugar	5 oz	142 g
Water	1½ fl oz	45 mL
Almonds, whole, blanched	1 lb	454 g
Butter	½ oz	14 g
Dark chocolate, melted, tempered	12 oz	340 g
Cocoa powder	½ oz	14 g

1. Combine the sugar and water in a heavy-bottomed saucepan and stir to ensure that all the sugar is moistened. Bring to a boil over high heat, stirring constantly. When the syrup comes to a boil, stop stirring and skim the surface to remove any scum. Continue to cook without stirring until the syrup reaches thread stage (215° to 230°F/102° to 110°C). Remove from the heat.

2. Immediately add the nuts and stir until the sugar crystallizes. Return to the heat and stir constantly until the sugar melts and caramelizes on the nuts.

3. Stir in the butter. Pour the mixture onto a marble slab and immediately separate the clusters of nuts. Allow to cool completely on the slab, then place in a bowl and chill for 3 minutes under refrigeration.

4. Add 4 oz/113 g of the tempered chocolate and stir (so the nuts don't stick together) until the chocolate sets. Repeat with another 4 oz/113 g chocolate. Add the remaining 4 oz/113 g chocolate and stir until it is almost set. Add the cocoa powder and stir to coat. Toss the nuts in a strainer to sift off the excess cocoa powder.

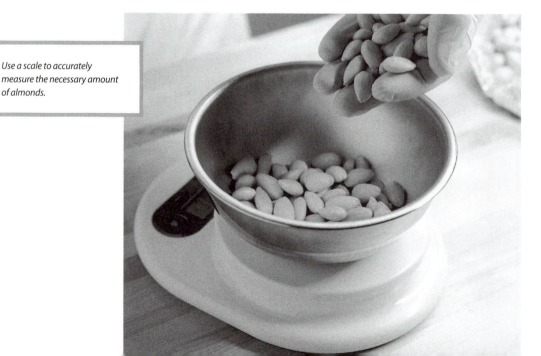

Use a scale to accurately measure the necessary amount of almonds.

3

CUTTING TOOLS AND TECHNIQUES

High-quality, well-made, well-maintained cutting tools are fundamental kitchen tools that form the foundation of a culinary professional's work. It is well worth spending the time and money necessary to acquire good knives and other cutting tools.

All cutting tools work best when they are properly maintained. A sharp tool not only performs better, but it is safer to use. Learn to sharpen knives with a stone and a steel so that you can maintain them yourself. Have severely dulled or damaged tools professionally reground to restore the edge.

Always carefully handle tools that cannot be resharpened, such as serrated knives, to extend their useful lives, and replace them as soon as they become difficult to use safely.

KNIVES

A knife should fit your hand, feel substantial but not too heavy, and be well-balanced. A true professional could get good—even great—results from a less-quality knife, but it is harder work. It is well worth spending the time and money necessary to acquire good knives and become comfortable with the skills involved in sharpening, steeling, and using them for a variety of cutting tasks.

Chef's/French Knife

This tool is the primary general-utility knife used in the kitchen. The all-purpose knife is good for chopping, mincing, and slicing. Chef's knives are usually available in 8-, 10-, and 12-inch/20-, 25- and 30-cm lengths with handles made from wood, steel, or synthetic materials. Blades can be made from carbon steel, stainless steel, ceramic, or a lamination of many different materials. Bakers use a chef's knife primarily for cutting fresh fruits and chopping chocolate and nuts.

Utility Knife

The utility knife is a size between the chef's knife and paring knife, ranging in length from 4 to 7 inches/10 to 18 cm. It is generally considered too fragile for heavier cutting tasks and is not well suited to fine tasks.

Paring Knife

This all-purpose knife is ideal for peeling and small intricate work. The length ranges from 2½ to 4 inches/6 to 10 cm. It can be used to cut small pieces of fruit, cut small garnishes, and make decorations for pastry, as well as to loosen cakes and other baked goods from their pans.

Serrated Bread Knife

This slicing knife has a long, thin, narrow blade, ranging from 8 to 12 inches in length. Look for a serrated knife made of high-carbon stain-resistant steel with a sturdy blade and a good handle. The scalloped teeth along the edge penetrate the surface without tearing or pulling, and protect the recessed cutting edge from getting dull.

The serrated bread knife is typically used for slicing crusty artisan breads and pastries with a spongy texture. In addition, this knife is excellent for slicing melons and citrus fruits, slicing peaches without bruising them, shaving chocolate, and cutting cake layers. Use a sawing motion to make smooth slices without crushing the product.

KNIFE SAFETY

Keep knives stored properly when not in use. There are a number of safe, practical ways to store knives, including slots, racks, and magnetized holders. Storage systems should be kept just as clean as the knives. After washing and sanitizing a knife, dry it completely before putting it away.

Always use the appropriate cutting surface. Wooden or composition cutting boards are best. Cutting on metal, glass, or marble surfaces will dull and eventually damage the blade and could lead to a dangerous slip of the knife.

To pass a knife safely to someone, present it with the handle toward the other person. Whenever you carry a knife from one area of the kitchen to another, hold the blade point down with the sharpened edge facing you. Ideally, you should sheathe or wrap the knife before walking anywhere with it.

LEFT TO RIGHT: Blade guards, steel, slicer, chef's knife, serrated bread knife, serrated utility knife, paring knife, scissors, (below) sharpening stone.

Fruit Salsa

MAKES 1 LB 14 OZ/851 G

INGREDIENT	U.S.	METRIC
Papaya, small dice	5 oz	142 g
Mango, small dice	5 oz	142 g
Honeydew melon, small dice	5 oz	142 g
Strawberries, small dice	5 oz	142 g
Passion fruit juice	1 fl oz	30 mL
Mint, finely chopped	1 tbsp	3 g
Amaretto liqueur	3 fl oz	90 mL
Orange juice	8 fl oz	240 mL
Sugar	3 oz	85 g

1. Combine the fruits, passion fruit juice, and mint. Set aside to macerate.

2. Combine the Amaretto, orange juice, and sugar and bring to a boil. Boil until reduced to 7 fl oz/210 mL. Cool to room temperature.

3. Gently blend the reduced liquid into the fruit.

4. Refrigerate until needed.

Use a chef's knife and a cutting board to dice fruit, such as this mango, for fruit salsa.

When you lay a knife down on a work surface, be sure that no part of it extends over the edge of the work surface. Also be sure that the blade is facing away from the edge of the work surface. Finally, never try to catch a falling knife.

SHARPENING AND HONING A KNIFE

The key to the proper and efficient use of any knife is making sure that it is sharp. A knife with a sharp blade always works better and more safely because it cuts easily. Knife blades are given an edge on a sharpening stone and maintained between sharpenings by honing them with a steel.

Sharpening stones are essential to the proper maintenance of knives. Sharpen the blade by passing its edge over the stone at a 20-degree angle. The grit—the degree of coarseness or fineness of the stone's surface—abrades the blade's edge, creating a sharp cutting edge. When sharpening a knife, always begin by using the coarsest surface of the stone, and then move on to the finer surfaces.

A stone with a fine grit should be used for boning knives and other tools that require an especially sharp edge. Most stones may be used either dry or moistened with water or mineral oil but the latter is preferred. Carborundum stones have a fine side and a medium side. Arkansas stones are available in several grades of fineness. Some consist of three stones of varying degrees of fineness mounted on a wheel. Diamond-impregnated stones are also available. Although they are expensive, some chefs prefer them because they feel these stones give a sharper edge.

Opinion is split about whether a knife blade should be run over a stone from heel to tip or tip to heel. Most chefs do agree that consistency in the direction of the stroke used to pass the blade over the stone is important.

Before using a stone, be sure that it is properly stabilized. No matter which method you use, keep the following guidelines in mind:

1. *Anchor the stone to keep it from slipping as you work. Place Carborundum or diamond stones on a damp cloth or rubber mat. A triple-faced stone is mounted on a rotating framework that can be locked into position so that it cannot move.*

2. *Lubricate the stone with mineral oil or water. Be consistent about the type of lubricant you use on your stone. Water or mineral oil helps reduce friction as you sharpen your knife. The heat caused by friction may not seem significant, but it can eventually harm the blade.*

3. *Begin sharpening the edge on the coarsest grit you require. The duller the blade, the coarser the grit should be.*

4. *Run the entire edge over the surface of the stone, keeping the pressure even on the knife. Hold the knife at the correct angle as you work. A 20-degree angle is suitable for chef's knives and knives with similar blades. You may need to adjust the angle by a few degrees to properly sharpen thinner blades such as slicers, or thicker blades such as cleavers.*

5. *Always sharpen the blade in the same direction. This ensures that the edge remains even and in proper alignment.*

6. *Make strokes of equal number and equal pressure on each side of the blade. Do not oversharpen the edge on coarse stones. After about ten strokes on each side of the blade, move on to the next finer grit.*

7. *Finish sharpening on the finest stone then wash and dry the knife thoroughly before using or storing it.*

Sharpening Method One

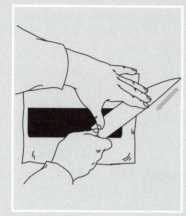

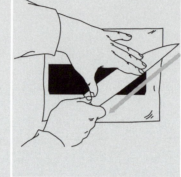

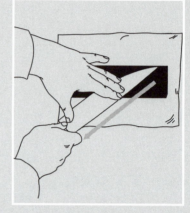

1 *Use four fingers of the guiding hand to maintain constant pressure on the knife.*

2 *Draw the knife across the stone gently.*

3 *Draw the knife off the stone smoothly. Turn the knife over and repeat the entire process on the other side.*

Sharpening Method Two

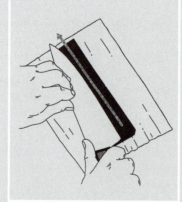

1 *Push the blade over the stone's surface, using the guiding hand to keep pressure even.*

2 *Continue to push the entire length of the blade over the stone.*

3 *Push the knife off the stone smoothly. Turn the knife over and repeat the entire process on the other side.*

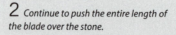

A steel should be used both immediately after sharpening the blade with a stone and also between sharpenings to keep the edge in alignment. The length of the steel's working surface can range from 3 inches for a pocket version to over 14 inches. Hard steel is the traditional material, but other materials, such as glass, ceramic, and diamond-impregnated surfaces, are also available. Steels come with coarse, medium, and fine grains, and some are magnetic, which helps the blade maintain proper alignment and also collects metal shavings.

When using a steel, hold the knife almost vertically, with the blade at a 20-degree angle, resting on the inner side of the steel. Draw the blade along the entire length of the steel.

KEEP THE FOLLOWING GUIDELINES IN MIND:

1. *Allow yourself plenty of room as you work, and stand with your weight evenly distributed. Hold the steel with your thumb and fingers safely behind the guard.*

2. *Draw the blade along the steel so that the entire edge touches the steel. Work in the same direction on each side of the blade to keep the edge straight.*

3. *Be sure to keep the pressure even to avoid wearing away the metal in the center of the edge. Over time, this could produce a curve in the edge. Keep the knife blade at a 20-degree angle to the steel.*

4. *Use a light touch, stroking evenly and consistently. Listen for a light ringing sound; a heavy grinding sound indicates that too much pressure is being applied.*

5. *Repeat the stroke on the opposite side of the edge to properly straighten the edge. If a blade requires more than five strokes per side on a steel to accomplish this, it probably should be sharpened on a stone.*

Steeling Method One

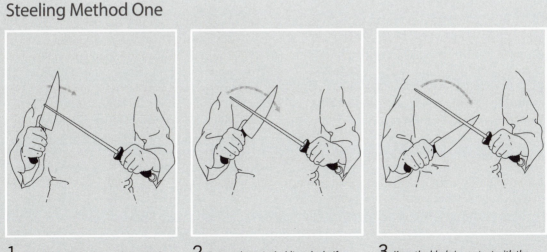

1 *Start with the knife nearly vertical, with the blade resting on the steel's inner side.*

2 *Rotate the wrist holding the knife as the blade moves along the steel in a downward motion.*

3 *Keep the blade in contact with the steel until the tip is drawn off the steel. Repeat the process with the blade resting on the steel's outer side.*

Steeling Method Two

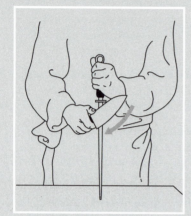

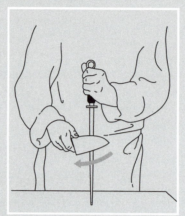

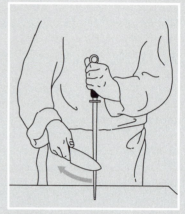

1 *Hold the steel in a near-vertical position with the tip resting on a nonslippery surface. Start with the heel of the knife against one side of the steel.*

2 *Maintain light pressure and use an arm action, not a wrist action, to draw the knife down the shaft of the steel in a smooth continuous motion.*

3 *Finish the first pass by drawing the blade all the way along the shaft up to and including the tip. Repeat the entire action, this time with the blade against the steel's other side.*

OTHER CUTTING TOOLS

Over time, specialized cutting tools have been designed to handle particular cutting tasks: Mandolines, kitchen shears, and guitars each fulfill a specific purpose in the bakeshop.

Mandoline

The mandoline is a slicing device made of stainless steel or plastic. It contains carbon-steel blades which can be adjusted to cut items of various shapes and thicknesses. This tool is also portable and folds flat for easy storage.

The advantage of utilizing a mandoline is that uniformity will be guaranteed; it results in very thin, very quick, even slices with very little effort. The food item is slid by hand along an adjustable surface until it meets the fixed blade, where it is sliced and falls through an opening. Slices, juliennes, and crinkle cuts can be made using the mandoline.

Great care should be taken as a mandoline can become extremely hazardous if the user moves too quickly or hastily.

Follow the manufacturer's instructions, properly use any safety guards, and use extreme care whenever cutting on a mandoline.

Kitchen Shears/Scissors

A sharp set of kitchen shears is a necessity for every baker. They can be used to cut plastic, acetate, string, wire, pastry dough, pulled sugar, and hard candies, to name a few things.

Purchase rust-proof kitchen shears, as they will need to be washed and dried often. The shears should have comfortable, nonslip handles for safety and should feel heavy and solidly constructed. If you are left-handed, purchase a left-handed model to ensure comfort.

Some kitchen shears have offset blades to allow the user to cut at an angle and still have leverage. The blades can also vary with serrated or straight edges, and blunt or softened tips. These blades will dull over time, but some models can be sharpened. Also, a sheath is recommended for safety.

Kitchen scissors are the most efficient tool to use when cutting marshmallows.

Marshmallows

MAKES 1 HALF SHEET PAN (13 BY 173/4 IN/33 BY 45 CM)

INGREDIENT	U.S.	METRIC
Gelatin, granulated	1¼ oz	35 g
Water, cold	16 fl oz	480 mL
Granulated sugar	1 lb 8 oz	680 g
Glucose syrup	12 oz	340 g
Honey	12 oz	340 g
Vanilla extract	1 tbsp	15 mL
Confectioners' sugar	As needed	

1. Line a half sheet pan with parchment paper.

2. Bloom the gelatin in 8 fl oz/240 mL of the cold water.

3. Combine the granulated sugar, glucose syrup, honey, and the remaining 8 fl oz/240 mL water in a heavy-bottomed saucepan and stir to ensure all the sugar is moistened. Bring to a boil over high heat, stirring to dissolve the sugar. When the syrup reaches a boil, stop stirring and skim the surface to remove any impurities.

4. Continue to cook without stirring, occasionally washing down the sides of the pan using a wet pastry brush, to 252°F/122°C. Remove from the heat and cool to approximately 210°F/99°C.

5. While the syrup is cooling, melt the gelatin over simmering water. Remove from the heat and stir in the vanilla.

6. Stir the gelatin mixture into the syrup. Whip the mixture on high speed with the whisk attachment until medium peaks form.

7. Spread the mixture evenly in the prepared sheet pan. The easiest way to do this is to place the mixture in the pan, place a sheet of oiled parchment paper on top, and roll out the marshmallow into the pan. Allow to set completely before unmolding and cutting.

8. Remove the slab from the pan, inverting it onto a work surface, and peel off the paper. Cut the marshmallows into 1-in/2.5-cm squares, dusting with confectioners' sugar as necessary.

Guitar

A guitar is a stainless-steel cutter that is used to precisely cut multiple squares, rectangles, triangles, or diamonds out of slabs of a variety of different semisoft confections, such as caramel and gelées.

It consists of a stainless steel square or rectangular platform with linear spaces that adjust to fit different sized, interchangeable cutting frames. The frames are threaded with stainless steel wire that cuts through the confections. Each set comes with at least three different sized cutting frames.

A guitar will easily cut confections, such as the gelée shown here, into bite-size pieces.

4

SMALL TOOLS AND APPLIANCES USAGE AND TECHNIQUES

The object of a specialized tool is to make the task at hand more efficient. A number of hand tools and small appliances belong in a culinary professional's repertoire. Particular preparations will dictate what tools are necessary, and individual bakers and pastry chefs will have their own particular likes and dislikes.

GRATERS, ZESTERS, AND RASPS

Grated, shredded, and zested food may be coarse or fine, depending on the intended use. To achieve the best result, it is important to choose the most appropriate grating tool.

Citrus Zester

The citrus zester is ideal for those who want to quickly remove zest from citrus fruits like oranges and lemons. The handheld tool has a stainless-steel edge with five tiny cutting holes and a handle. It is pulled across the surface of a citrus fruit to create threadlike strips of the peel. The advantage of the citrus zester is that it removes only the zest, leaving behind the bitter and pale pith.

Microplane Grater

This handheld version of a box grater is made of stainless steel and has a plastic handle. The Microplane grater is good for citrus zest, hard cheeses, fresh ginger, and coconut. It can also be used to create small chocolate shavings for garnish on cakes and individual desserts. The metal perforations gently shred away pieces of the item, producing the lightest and finest zest. The openings can range from very fine and small for grating spices like nutmeg, to large for hard cheeses. The Microplane grater is ideal for citrus zesting because it leaves behind the bitter pith.

Nutmeg Grater

The nutmeg grater is a handheld tool used for grating or grinding spices. It comes in two varieties:

one with a metal section for grating on the outside, and one with a handle to turn a grating mechanism inside the tool. The grater can be made from clear acrylic, stainless steel, or chrome and comes in a cylindrical or round shape. Most nutmeg graters also have a compartment to store whole nutmeg.

In addition to grating nutmeg, the grater can be used for grating cinnamon sticks, garlic cloves, lemon rind, chocolate, fresh ginger, and even some hard cheeses like aged Cheddar or and Parmigiano-Reggiano.

PEELERS AND CORERS

Some fruits and vegetables require preliminary trimming, peeling, or coring to remove inedible portions or make subsequent cuts easier to perform. Chef's or paring knives may be used for these applications, but peelers, corers, and pitting tools are specialized to help complete the job more quickly, more cleanly, and with less waste.

Swivel-Blade Peeler

A swivel blade peeler can be used to easily peel tough-skinned mangos and papayas, as well as shave the zest of lemons, limes, and oranges. The serrated or straight stainless-steel blade rotates slightly to follow the contours of the food item and remove a thin layer of skin. The sharp end, called an *eyer,* is used for removing blemishes.

Corer

The corer is a cylinder with a sharpened end and a handle on the other end. When it is placed over the

Lemon Curd

MAKES 2 LB 2 OZ/964 G

INGREDIENT	U.S.	METRIC
Butter, cubed	1 lb 5 oz	596 g
Sugar	1 lb 2 oz	510 g
Lemon juice	18 fl oz	540 mL
Lemon zest, grated	1¼ oz	35 g
Egg yolks	1 lb 2 oz	510 g

1. Combine 10½ oz/298 g of the butter, 9 oz/255 g of the sugar, and the lemon juice and zest and bring to a boil over medium heat, stirring gently to dissolve the sugar.

2. Blend the egg yolks with the remaining 9 oz/255 g sugar. Temper by gradually adding about one-third of the lemon juice mixture, stirring constantly with a whisk. Return the tempered egg mixture to the saucepan. Continue cooking, stirring constantly with the whisk, until the mixture comes to a boil.

3. Stir in the remaining 10½ oz/298 g butter.

4. Strain the curd into a large shallow container or bowl. Cover with plastic wrap placed directly on the surface of the curd. Cool over an ice water bath.

5. Store the curd, covered, under refrigeration until ready to serve.

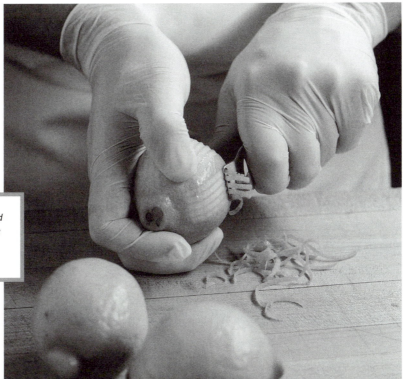

When zesting citrus fruits, avoid going too deeply into the white pith below the peel, which can have a bitter flavor.

center of a fruit, the user can push down to force the sharp end into the fruit, cutting out the core. When the corer is pulled out of the fruit, it takes the core with it, leaving only the edible parts of the fruit behind.

A corer is usually made of heavy-duty stainless steel and has a sturdy, easy to grip handle. Removing the core of fruits like apples and pears is ideal for desserts like pies and tarts. There is also another model available which has two handles and about eight sectional blades. When pressed into the fruit, it removes the core and divides the fruit into even, uniform pieces. This tool is ideal for those who want to quickly cut apples for pies or canning purposes.

Cherry Pitter

A cherry pitter is a handheld spring-loaded tool that extracts the pit from a cherry while leaving the fruit whole. Cherry pitters may be stainless steel, aluminum, or plastic. Cherry pitters can also be used to pit fresh whole olives.

SIFTERS AND STRAINERS

Sifters and strainers are used to sift, aerate, and help remove large impurities from dry ingredients. They may also be used to drain or purée cooked or raw foods. The delicate mesh of some strainers is highly vulnerable to damage, so never drop these into a pot sink where they could be crushed or torn.

Strainers

Strainers are used to separate liquids from solids. They are made of wire mesh and sometimes have a handle. Some strainers have larger holes for straining bubbles or filtering ingredients. Others are used to create lump-free batters and sauces.

Drum Sieve/Tamis

A drum sieve or tamis is wire mesh sandwiched between two round stainless-steel hoop frames. The sieve is wide and flat to allow for dry ingredients like flours and sugars to be pushed through in a flat, non-tiring motion. These are also useful tools to help with refining texture since ingredients are broken into smaller pieces when passed through the wire mesh.

Conical Sieves

Conical sieves are typically made of stainless steel and can come with a handle or without. The conical shape allows the sieve to rest inside a tall container like a bain-marie. These will often have a mesh screen and can sit inside liquid measuring cups.

Colander

A colander is a tool used to wash and dry items like fruits. It can be made of plastic or stainless steel and looks like a wide bowl with perforated holes and one or two handles. Sometimes a pedestal or ring is attached to the base to allow the colander to stand on its own.

Cheesecloth

Cheesecloth is a loosely woven cotton cloth that in addition to cheese making is useful for separating solids and liquids. The cloth is neutral, imparting no flavors, which is a positive characteristic. It is also available in several grades, ranging from open to extra-fine weaves. Cheesecloth can be reused but will break down eventually.

Before the first use, cheesecloth should be dampened to allow easier passage of liquids. It can be used to strain custards, sauces, coulis, and jellies. Cheesecloth is also good for bundling herbs or teas for steeping or infusing sauces and poaching liquids.

CLOCKWISE FROM TOP: Tamis, conical sieve, cheesecloth (on bottom), strainer, colander.

SPOONS AND TONGS

A professional-quality kitchen spoon may have a solid, slotted, or perforated head and may be made from metal, heatproof plastic, or wood. Spoons are used for stirring, mixing, and serving. Similarly, tongs are used to grip a food item firmly enough to lift, turn, mix, or serve it.

Slotted/Perforated Spoons

A spoon with slots, holes, or other openings in the bowl section of the spoon is called a *slotted* or *perforated spoon*. It acts as a ladle and sieve at once; liquid passes through the holes, keeping the larger solids in the spoon. It can be made of stainless steel, wood, or plastic.

A slotted spoon is useful for removing poached fruit from syrup, fritters and doughnuts from hot oil, and for portioning compotes.

Wooden Spoons

One of the most common kitchen tools is the wooden spoon. It can be used to cream together butter and sugar by hand as well as for mixing and folding in fruits, chocolate, and nuts. One benefit of the wooden spoon is that it does not transfer heat, making it ideal to use when stirring cooked custards and puddings. The wood also does not scratch saucepans. Wooden spoons come in a variety of sizes. Choose one with a sturdy handle and maintain it by scrubbing the spoon with some mineral oil.

Spiders/Skimmers

Spiders or skimmers consist of a long handle with a wire woven basket at the end. The basket is made of stainless steel and can be either flat or round. Spiders are useful for retrieving cooked foods from hot water or oil, such as doughnuts, poached fruits, fritters, and candied nuts.

Tongs

Kitchen tongs are a versatile grasping device made of stainless steel that can help protect hands from burns as well as extend reach. They can be purchased in two sizes: long and short. In addition to using tongs for serving at buffets, they can be used to rotate cakes and pies in the oven and remove food from a hot fryer.

LEFT TO RIGHT: Perforated skimmer, tongs, metal spoon, slotted spoon, wooden spoons, spider.

WHISKS

Whisks, also called whips, are made from a number of thin wires bound together with a handle. Whisks are used to blend or whisk ingredients, to loosen and evenly distribute ingredients, and to make foams such as whipped cream and meringue.

Balloon Whisks

The balloon whisk was designed to incorporate as much air as possible into egg whites and cream. Whisks can range in length from 8 to 18 inches with thin looped wires forming an elongated shape.

More wires on the balloon whisk will increase the whisk's contact area and the speed of the process.

Flat Whisks

A flat whisk is composed of four or five wires lying flat, about 3 to 4 inches/7.5 to 10 cm wide and 10 to 12 inches/25 to 30 cm long. A stainless-steel whisk with a heat-resistant handle is best for mixing hot sauces in low pans. The flat whisk can also be used to lightly beat eggs in a shallow bowl, incorporate flour into melted butter, stir custards and chocolate sauces, and scrape ingredients out of bowls.

LEFT TO RIGHT: Flat whisk, silicone balloon whisk, three styles of metal balloon whisks.

SPATULAS AND SCRAPERS

Spatulas and scrapers are available in several different configurations but essentially consist of a broad, flat head or blade attached to a handle. Spatulas with a metal blade, which may be straight or offset, are used to turn or lift foods and can be used when spreading icings and batters. Spatulas with a flexible head made of rubber or silicon, sometimes referred to as rubber scrapers, are used to fold batters, spread soft foods, and scrape out the contents of pans, bowls, and other containers cleanly.

Rubber Spatulas

The rubber spatula is one of the most invaluable baking tools. It has a near-rectangle end made of synthetic rubber which will conform to the sides of any bowl. Some rubber spatulas are made of high-temperature-resistant synthetic rubber that is able to withstand temperatures of 300°F/149°C or higher. They also will not stain, curl, or absorb food odors. Rubber spatulas come in a variety of sizes, as well as shapes (flat or spoon-shaped). They are useful for folding eggs and foams into heavier bases as well as scraping batters out of bowls.

LEFT TO RIGHT: Large offset metal spatula, flat metal spatula, small offset metal spatula, plastic bowl scraper, rubber spoon-spatula, rubber spatula.

Metal Spatulas

Metal baking spatulas are like an extension of your hands and fingers; they are good for spreading batter into corners, leveling cakes with frosting and glazes, and finishing pastries. The straight variety is excellent for supporting cakes while being moved, and for leveling the tops of cakes. An offset metal spatula is bent near the handle and can be used to lift many cookies or pastries at once. They come in a variety of sizes and shapes. The wedge-shaped offset spatula can be used to serve pieces of cake and pie. The small and narrow offset spatula is ideal for spreading frosting on cupcakes and picking up small, delicate pastry items.

Plastic Bowl Scraper

A plastic bowl scraper is a D-shaped piece of plastic used to provide a little more control than a regular spatula. Made of stiff plastic, it is flexible enough to wedge items out of a pan, yet stiff enough to pick up batter. The curved edge can be used to remove batter and dough from a bowl and the flat edge can be used to smooth the surface of batter before baking.

A plastic bowl scraper is also useful because it will lift and scrape foods from pans without scratching, and it can be used to help sift and push purées through a tamis or strainer.

Bench Scraper

A bench scraper is a straight-edged rectangle of stainless steel with an ample handle on top. It is also known as a *bench knife*. This tool was designed to scrape dough off a baker's bench, but has many other uses. It is good for portioning bread doughs, cookie doughs, and other pastry items. A bench scraper can be used to scrape, lift, and cut, and is extremely useful in candy making as sugar does not stick to the metal.

SCOOPS AND LADLES

Scoops and ladles come in a wide variety of sizes and may be used to portion foods, such as ice cream, for service, or to portion out batters and doughs for baking.

Ice Cream Scoops

Ice cream scoops are good for making equal portions of any soft to semisoft food, such as ice cream, sorbet, truffles, and cookies. The scoops can be oval or round in shape, range in diameter from 1½ to 3 inches/3.75 to 7.5 mL, and are made of stainless steel. Some scoops have sturdy plastic handles as well.

Insulated scoops are popular. The handles contain a salt-based fluid, which is activated by body heat. This warms the scoop up, helping to easily release frozen items.

There are also hinged scoops available. A cog-regulated spring-release blade moves in the scoop after the user releases a coiled spring attached to the grip.

Melon Ballers

Also known as a *Parisian scoop,* the melon baller can be used to create neat, rounded balls or ovals. The handheld tool has a wooden, metal, or plastic handle and a large and small stainless-steel scoop on either end. The edges can be straight or fluted, and each scoop has a small hole that allows air and juices to pass through. A melon baller is used for items that are soft enough to scoop but firm enough to hold their shape.

This tool can be used to form tiny truffles, butter pats, and fruit garnishes. It also facilitates easy removal of apple and pear cores, leaving neat, rounded hollows. Ice cream and sorbet can be scooped with the melon baller and be used for garnishes or small tastes.

To use, press down firmly and twist to shape a perfect ball or oval.

Portioning Scoops

Portioning scoops are used to portion out batters and doughs. Mechanical scoops have a lever to operate a blade that sweeps over the inside of the scoop's bowl to release the food from the scoop. Scoops are made in a variety of standard sizes that are numbered according to their volume. The higher the number, the smaller the volume; so, for example, a #16 scoop makes larger cookies than a #30 or #24 scoop.

Ladles

A ladle is a calibrated cup with a long, broad handle. Ladles come in a range of sizes, from 1- to 2- to 4-fluid ounce/30- to 60- to 120-mL portions or larger with varying lengths of handles. Oftentimes handles will have a curved hook at the end to hang them up for storage. Ladles are useful for serving even portions, transferring fluid batter, and portioning sauces for plated desserts.

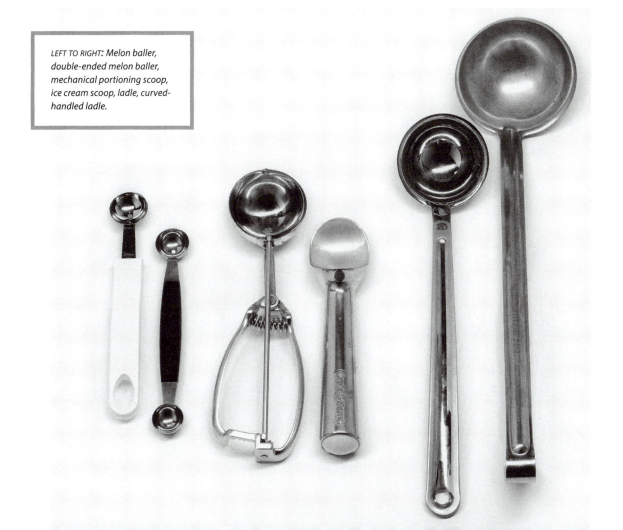

LEFT TO RIGHT: Melon baller, double-ended melon baller, mechanical portioning scoop, ice cream scoop, ladle, curved-handled ladle.

COOLING RACKS

Wire racks are useful in allowing air to pass through and around hot products to cool them down quickly. In addition to assisting cooling, wire racks can be used as glazing screens when pouring a soft ganache or glaze over cakes and cookies. They are composed of stainless steel or nonstick wires that are interwoven in a large or small weave. Wire racks come in a variety of shapes: rectangular, square, and circular, and some have collapsible legs.

GRINDING, PURÉEING, AND CHOPPING TOOLS AND APPLIANCES

Food Mill

A food mill is a large stainless-steel bowl with a crank, curved blades, and a perforated disk which forces food through the holes. Most have a 2-quart/1.92 L capacity. The food mill separates as it purées, leaving seeds and skins behind. Usually, there are three interchangeable blades that allow the user to produce purées of varying textures. This tool is ideal for fruit soups, sauces, coulis, and fillings.

Coffee and Spice Mills

Coffee and spice mills are very useful for grinding small quantities of nuts, coffee beans, chocolate, and spices. This allows the baker to have freshly ground ingredients.

Mortars and Pestles

Along with the knife, the mortar and pestle is one of the most basic tools in our repertoire. There are two parts to this hand-powered grinding tool: the mortar, a concave surface like a bowl that holds the food, and the pestle, a rod with a curved end that is pressed and rubbed against the food. The mortar and pestle are used to grind almost any foodstuff to a desired texture. The great appeal of this tool is the way it lets you control the texture of the food as precisely as you can control its flavor.

Dating back to the Stone Age, the mortar and pestle has developed into a range of styles, according to the materials available and the types of grinding tasks important in a particular cuisine. For example, the Mexican *metate y metlapil* is a device traditionally used to grind flour in which the mortar is a curved plate and the pestle is a bellowed rolling pin, while the Japanese *suribachi* is a textured earthenware bowl with a wooden dowel called a *surikogi*. Other variations of the mortar and pestle are found throughout Europe and Thailand.

Blender

The blender is an appliance used to mix ingredients or purée food, among other things. It is composed of a housing, motor, blades, and food container. The food container looks like a pitcher with a base that fits into the housing. It is typically made of glass, plastic, and stainless steel. Oftentimes there are graduated markings on the side of the food container to assist in measuring. A lid fits on top of the container to prevent ingredients from escaping. At the bottom is a rotating blade. The container base locks onto the housing with a twist and the blender is operated by the push of a button.

LEFT TO RIGHT: Food mill, spice grinder, mortar and pestle.

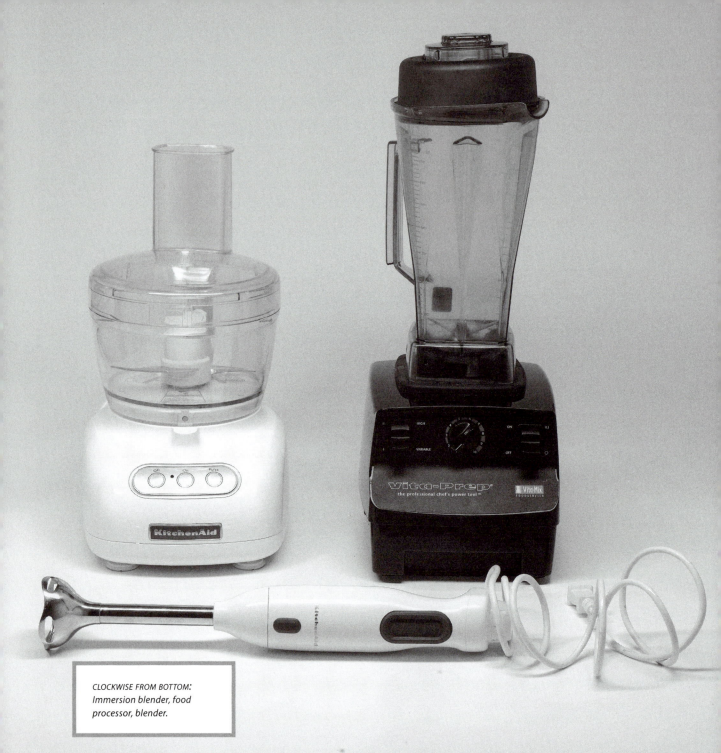

CLOCKWISE FROM BOTTOM:
Immersion blender, food
processor, blender.

A blender can mix, whip, emulsify, crush, and blend ingredients together. Ice can be crushed for use in smoothies and cocktails. A good, high-powered blender can mill grains, reducing items like spices and seeds to powder or nut butter.

Immersion Blender

Unlike a standard blender, the immersion blender has no food container. It is composed of a housing, motor, and mixing head with rotating blades and can be operated with one hand.

When using an immersion blender, the blade should be kept immersed in the liquid and should be used in containers with high sides to prevent ingredients from escaping the container.

Food Processor

A food processor is short and wide and, unlike a blender, does not need liquid to facilitate movement. The transparent plastic food container is locked onto the base and the lid often has a mechanical safety device so the machine cannot be used while the lid is open or off. This appliance comes in sizes ranging from mini to full.

The blade is interchangeable and many disks or attachments are available, such as a dough blade, an egg whisk, a julienne disk, and a citrus juicer. The most common blade is S-shaped and referred to as a *sabatier blade*.

A food processor is useful for slicing, chopping, puréeing, grinding, shredding, and mixing. It can be used to make marzipan, gianduja, nut butter, and pie dough.

MIXERS

Mixers are electric machines used to mix, beat, whip, or knead a batter or dough. Mixers are available in a variety of sizes to handle various capacities and can be fitted with paddle, whisk, or dough hook attachments. Mixers have the potential to be extremely dangerous. The importance of observing all the necessary safety precautions cannot be overemphasized. Proper maintenance and cleaning should also be performed consistently in order to keep the equipment in good working order and prevent injury.

Planetary Mixer

A planetary mixer is also known as a *vertical mixer* or *stand mixer*. It gets its name from the motion of the mixing attachment in the stationary mixing bowl—a path that is like that of a planet rotating on its axis while revolving around the sun. The mixer comes with three standard attachments—a paddle, a whisk, and a dough hook—and has multiple uses.

Spiral Mixer

A spiral mixer is a stationary mixer, meaning that the bowl, rather than the mixing attachment, rotates. The mixer has a bowl that tilts and only one attachment, a spiral-shaped hook. It is used exclusively for mixing bread doughs. It works the dough quickly but gently enough to control the amount of friction.

Oblique Mixer

An oblique mixer, also known as a *fork mixer*, is similar in construction to a spiral mixer except that the attachment is a fork rather than a spiral. It is also used exclusively for bread doughs and works the dough gently to minimize the amount of friction, as does a spiral mixer.

Vertical mixer.

Sabayon

MAKES 32 FL OZ/960 ML

INGREDIENT	U.S.	METRIC
Egg yolks	12 oz	340 g
Sugar	12 oz	340 g
White wine	12 fl oz	360 mL

1. Combine the egg yolks, sugar, and wine in the bowl of a mixer and whip together with the whisk attachment until thoroughly blended. Place the bowl over simmering water and heat, whisking constantly, until the mixture is thickened and very foamy and has reached 180°F/82°C.

2. Transfer the bowl back to the mixer and whip on high speed with the whisk attachment until cool.

3. Transfer the sabayon to a container and cover it with plastic wrap placed directly against the surface to prevent a skin from forming. Sabayon may be served warm or at room temperature.

Whip the sabayon on high speed in a stand mixer fitted with a whisk attachment until it is cool.

ICE CREAM MACHINES

An ice cream machine is a specialized piece of equipment used to cool and churn a liquid base into ice cream. Models range from very simple hand-cranked versions to huge commercial machines with built-in refrigeration.

Hand-Cranked Ice Cream Machine

The simple hand-cranked ice cream machine has a handle that you must crank to turn the paddle within the cooling chamber or rotate the chamber around the paddle. The machine can ordinarily produce up to a quart of ice cream per batch.

Electric Ice Cream Machine

An electric ice cream machine has a motor that either turns the paddle within the cooling chamber or rotates the chamber around the paddle. The bowl is usually removable and must be frozen for at least 12 hours before use. Bowls range from 6 to 9 inches/ 15 to 22.5 cm in diameter and up to 6½ inches/ 16.25 cm tall. The machine can ordinarily produce up to a quart of ice cream per batch.

Commercial Ice Cream Freezers

Commercial ice cream makers have built-in refrigeration units to make large-scale production of ice cream and other frozen confections possible. There are two basic types: continuous and batch.

With a continuous ice cream freezer, the ice cream base is fed continuously into the machine at a high rate of speed. This type of machine allows for control of overrun, viscosity, and temperature of the finished product.

Batch ice cream freezers are available in two basic configurations: horizontal and vertical. The horizontal machine has a cylinder that lies horizontally within the unit. It incorporates a considerable amount of air into the product. The vertical machine has a vertical cylinder within the unit for churning and freezing the base. It incorporates the least amount of air into the product as the mix is scraped and blended.

JUICERS

There are several options when it comes to juicing fruits and vegetables. Freshly juicing seasonal produce is a great way to flavor cakes, sauces, icings, and other products.

Reamer

Also known as a citrus reamer, this basic tool quickly and efficiently juices small citrus fruits. Reamers are traditionally carved wood, but may also be plastic or metal. On one end is a handle and on the other is a convexly conical end with deep troughs along the sides and a smooth spike on the tip.

After the citrus fruit is sliced in half, use the tip of the reamer to remove any visible seeds. Pierce the flesh with the reamer, then grind from the inside out in a twisting motion to extract all the juice. The juice should be strained before use to remove any remaining seeds.

The reamer is prized for its simple design. It is a safe, durable tool with a high yield that is easy to clean, readily available, and very affordable.

Crank Juicer

A crank juicer is a manual machine that may sit on the tabletop or mount on the edge of a table. A crank juicer may be made of heavy duty plastic or metal and can be totally disassembled for cleaning. It can be used to juice a variety of fruits and vegetables, but they will need to be peeled and/or cut into small pieces (because the manual machine is not as powerful as its electric counterpart).

To use a crank juicer, place the item to be juiced into the chute in the top of the machine, turn the manual crank, and the juice is expressed out the bottom.

Electric Juicer

An electric juicer is the most expensive but most powerful type of juicer. It is also the fastest and least labor-intensive. To use an electric juicer, place the item to be juiced into the chute in the top of the machine and just press a button. Depending on the make of the juicer, the juice may be expressed out a spout at the bottom of the machine or collected in a removable compartment within the machine.

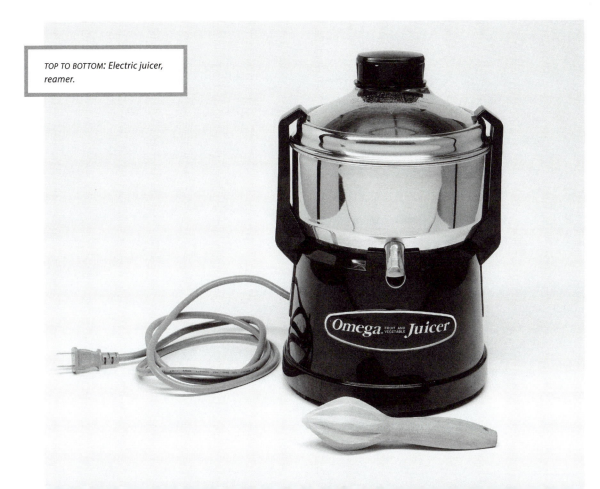

TOP TO BOTTOM: Electric juicer, reamer.

BLOWTORCH

A small butane or propane torch can be an invaluable piece of equipment in a pastry kitchen. A handheld torch gives you control that you do not have with a broiler. A torch can be used to finish crème brûlée and other desserts that require a caramelized exterior and to give color to baked fruit or meringue topping.

Carefully use a blowtorch to caramelize the sugar on top of each crème brûlée.

Crème Brûlée

INGREDIENT	U.S.	METRIC
BRÛLÉE SUGAR BLEND		
Granulated sugar	8 oz	227 g
Light brown sugar	8 oz	227 g
Heavy cream	32 fl oz	960 mL
Granulated sugar	6 oz	170 g
Salt	Pinch	
Vanilla bean	1 each	1 each
Egg yolks, beaten	5½ oz	156 g
Brûlée sugar blend	5 oz	142 g
Confectioners' sugar, for dusting	4½ oz	128 g

1. To make the brûlée sugar blend: Combine the two sugars and spread out on a sheet pan. Allow to dry overnight. Process the sugar mixture in a food processor until very fine. Sift through a fine-mesh strainer.

2. Combine the cream, 3 oz/85 g of the granulated sugar, and the salt in a nonreactive saucepan and bring to a simmer over medium heat, stirring gently with a wooden spoon. Remove from the heat.

Split the vanilla bean lengthwise, scrape the seeds from the pod. Add both the seeds and the pod to the pan, cover, and steep for 15 minutes.

3. Bring the cream to a boil.

4. Blend the egg yolks with the remaining 3 oz/85 g granulated sugar. Temper by gradually adding about one-third of the hot cream, stirring constantly with a whisk. Add the remaining hot cream. Strain and ladle into ramekins, filling them three-quarters full.

5. Bake the custards in a water bath at 325°F/163°C until just set, 20 to 25 minutes.

6. Remove the custards from the water bath and wipe the ramekins dry. Refrigerate until fully chilled.

7. To finish the crème brûlée: Evenly coat each custard's surface with a thin layer (1/16 in/1.5 mm) of the brûlée sugar blend. Use a blowtorch to melt and caramelize the sugar. Lightly dust the surface with confectioners' sugar and serve.

DOUGH SHEETER

The dough sheeter is a machine that accepts pieces of irregularly shaped dough and rolls them to a uniform thickness. The dough is placed on a canvas conveyor belt that is moved back and forth between rollers several times. After each pass, the space between the rollers is adjusted and decreased until the desired thickness has been reached.

This machine is ideal for puff pastry, pie crust, lavash, pizza dough, and fondant. The dough sheeter eliminates the need for hand rolling, is fast, efficient and consistent, and increases production levels.

Dough sheeter.

MOLDER

A bread molder is a machine with adjustable, spring-loaded rollers that roll and form dough into uniform shapes. Some machines require the dough to be hand-fed while others are automated as part of an assembly line operation. Molders may be used to shape baguettes, loaves, and rolls.

PROOFER

For a professional bread baker in a high-volume operation, a proofer is an essential piece of equipment. Proofers maintain the most desirable environment for yeast growth. In this way, they help to maintain production schedules and ensure that items are

Proofer.

of uniform quality. Some proofers have refrigeration capabilities, making them able to retard yeast growth. Proofers like this are known as *proofer/ retarders*. Retarders also help with production in the same ways as a proofer, by maintaining production schedules and quality standards. They are available as stationary walk-ins or as mobile boxes.

RETARDER

Retarding means purposely cooling a dough in order to slow the fermentation process. A retarder is a cabinet-style machine that will maintain the dough at a set temperature, typically around 40°F/4°C. Retarding dough allows bakers to organize their work to meet production and employee schedules and also gives the gluten in the dough more time to relax, resulting in dough that is easier to shape. In the case of doughs made using direct fermentation, retarding gives the dough more time to develop a pronounced sour flavor and therefore results in a better quality dough.

5

BREAD BAKING AND QUICK-BREAD MAKING TECHNIQUES AND TOOLS

Breads and rolls made from yeast-raised doughs and batters have a distinct aroma and flavor, but the final products vary from the simplicity of a hearth-baked pizza to a delicate egg- and butter-enriched brioche. Unlike other breads, quick breads are generally leavened with chemical leaveners, such as baking powder, rather than yeast.

BREADS

A high-quality bread dough is dependent on the flour, water, salt, and yeast being worked together in the correct proportions for the appropriate amount of time and at the proper temperature. The way in which yeast is introduced into a bread dough—by either direct or indirect fermentation—gives a bread baker the range of techniques necessary to create simple lean dough quickly and efficiently as well as to create hearty breads using more complex methods, such as sponges, bigas, and sourdoughs.

Basic Yeast Dough Steps

1 First, in the pick-up period, the ingredients are blended on low speed until just combined. The dough is a rough mass at this point. Next, during the cleanup period, or preliminary development, the dough is mixed at a moderate speed and appears somewhat rough.

2 The development period is marked by the dough beginning to pull away from the sides of the mixing bowl, which indicates the development of the gluten's elasticity. Lastly, during final gluten development, the dough is smooth and elastic and leaves the sides of the bowl completely clean as the mixer is running.

3 The first fermentation period, known as bulk fermentation, develops the flavor of the bread. The mixed dough is transferred to a lightly oiled bowl and covered to prevent a skin from forming on the surface.

4 The dough is rested at room temperature (75°F/24°C) until it has doubled in size.

Fermentation

Fermentation is a process that happens in any dough containing yeast. As the yeast eats the sugars present in the dough, carbon dioxide is released, which causes the dough to expand. It begins as soon as the ingredients are mixed together and continues until the dough reaches an internal temperature of 138°F/59°C during baking. The carbon dioxide acts to leaven a dough or batter as the gas is trapped in the web of protein (gluten) strands that developed during the mixing process. The alcohol created through fermentation acts to tenderize the gluten strands, improving the overall texture of the product; it cooks out during baking, leaving no undesirable flavor.

5 Dough is folded over during or after bulk fermentation to redistribute the available food supply for the yeast, equalize the temperature of the dough, expel the built-up fermentation gases, and further develop the gluten in the dough. The dough should be folded over carefully to preserve the already developed structure.

6 Accurate scaling creates uniformity of size for each dough piece, which allows for uniformity in proofing and baking times.

After scaling, the dough is gently preshaped into a round or oblong. Preshaping gives the dough a smooth, tight skin that will help trap the gases that develop during fermentation. Resting for 10 to 20 minutes covered with a linen cloth or plastic wrap after preshaping allows the gluten to relax, so that the dough is easier to manipulate into its final shape.

After resting, the dough is given is final shape.

7 After shaping, the dough undergoes one more fermentation. Some doughs, such as the lean dough used to prepare boules, can simply be placed on a worktable or a board that has been dusted with flour or cornmeal. Other doughs or shapes may be placed on a couche (linen cloth) or sheet pans, in loaf pans, or in baskets (bannetons), wooden molds, or other molds.

The fermentation process is important in building the internal structure and flavor of the dough. Given the proper environment, yeast cells will continue to ferment until they run out of food, or until the by-products of fermentation begin to poison them and they die, or they are baked to the correct internal temperature. There are several types of fermentation, all of which have different purposes and yield different results.

DIRECT FERMENTATION

The simplest and fastest method for producing a lean dough is direct fermentation: Commercially produced yeast is combined with flour, water, and salt and mixed until the dough is supple and elastic with well-developed gluten. Flour, as a main component, provides the structure and crumb in breads through the action of the proteins and starches it contains. The amount of water or other liquids also has an impact on the finished loaf. As the amount of liquid in a dough increases, the bread's structure changes as it promotes the formation of an open crumb. The direct fermentation method of bread making requires fewer steps and less advance preparation than indirect fermentation methods.

Bulk Fermentation

The first fermentation period, known as bulk fermentation, develops the flavor of bread. Bulk fermentation is especially important when using the direct fermentation method; without the addition of pre-ferments, this is the only time to develop flavor through fermentation. Regulating the temperature may extend the time or rate of fermentation during this period. Keeping the dough at cooler temperatures will result in a longer fermentation period and thus more flavor development. The properly mixed dough is transferred to a lightly oiled bowl or tub (stiff or firm doughs can be placed on a lightly floured tabletop). The dough is covered with a moist cloth or plastic wrap to prevent a skin from forming on the surface and it is rested at the appropriate temperature until it has doubled in size.

Resting or Intermediate Fermentation

After bulk fermentation and the dividing and pre-shaping of the dough, it is allowed to ferment again. This period has various names: bench rest, table rest, or secondary or immediate fermentation. This stage allows the dough to relax and recover from the dividing and preshaping process in preparation for final shaping: It allows the gluten to relax, so the dough will become somewhat slack and easier to manipulate into its final shape, and it allows the yeast cells to recover, rebuilding carbon dioxide and therefore the internal structure of the dough. Normally, this stage lasts from 10 to 20 minutes.

Final Fermentation (Proofing)

After shaping, the dough undergoes one more fermentation. Some doughs can simply be placed on a worktable or a board that has been dusted with flour or cornmeal. Other doughs or shapes may be placed on a linen cloth (couche), on sheet pans, in loaf pans, or in baskets (bannetons), wooden molds, or other molds. During the final rise, it is again important to ensure that a skin does not form on the surface of the dough. If you are not using a proof box for this final proof, the dough should be covered. Using the temperature and humidity controls in a proof box will prevent a skin from forming without the dough being covered.

Small items such as rolls must be allowed to fully ferment during the final proofing because they bake quickly, leaving less time for fermentation in the oven. Large items such as loaves should be proofed to a slightly less developed state than small items, as they require longer baking times and will continue to ferment (or proof) for a longer time in the oven.

INDIRECT FERMENTATION AND PRE-FERMENTS

Indirect fermentation means that some portion of the dough is allowed to ferment on its own before being mixed with the remainder of the formula's ingredients. This portion, often referred to as a pre-ferment, typically includes only flour, water (or milk), and some or all of the yeast called for in the final dough. The longer the yeast in a dough remains active, the better the flavor and texture of the finished bread will be.

It is important to plan for pre-ferments in a production schedule. The time requirement for each type of pre-ferment is slightly different, as noted below.

Pâte Fermentée

Pâte fermentée, or "old dough," is nothing more exotic than a piece of a lean wheat dough reserved from the previous day's production. The dough is covered and refrigerated until needed, then added along with the other ingredients to make a batch of dough. The yeast in the pâte fermentée has undergone an extended fermentation and has developed an appealing, slightly sour flavor.

Sponge

This pre-ferment combines one-third to one-half of the formula's total flour with all the yeast and enough liquid to make a stiff to loose dough. The sponge can be made directly in the mixing bowl, as the fermenta-

tion period is typically less than one hour. When the sponge has doubled in size, the remaining ingredients are mixed in to make the final dough.

Poolish

A poolish combines equal parts flour and water (by weight) with some yeast (the amount varies according to the expected length of fermentation time, using less yeast for longer, slower fermentations). The poolish is fermented at room temperature long enough to double in volume and start to recede, or decrease, in volume. This may take anywhere from 3 to 15 hours depending on the amount of yeast. The poolish should be mixed in a plastic or other nonreactive container large enough to hold the mixture comfortably as it ferments.

Biga

Biga is the stiffest of the pre-ferments. It contains flour and enough water to equal 50 to 60 percent of the flour's weight, as well as 0.33 to 0.5 percent of the formula's total yeast. After the biga has properly fermented, it must be loosened with a portion of the formula's liquid to make it easier to blend into the dough.

Sourdough Starter

A sourdough starter adds flavor to breads, and in some formulas that may be its primary function. But sourdough is a true leavener. Although it is time-consuming to prepare and maintain a sourdough starter to be used as a primary leavener, breads made with sourdough have a deep, complex flavor and a good texture. A sourdough is acidic enough to enhance the shelf life of breads and rolls. A strong, vigorous sourdough can be maintained indefinitely with proper feedings.

Each sourdough has its own characteristics, depending on both the ingredients selected and the type of wild yeasts in any given environment. Both wheat and rye flours are used in sourdough starters. Wheat flours generate lactic acid; rye develops acetic acid. These acids influence the flavor of the finished bread. Organic flours are easiest to use for starters since they are minimally processed and do not contain the additives found in nonorganic flours.

ESTABLISHING A STARTER

The initial stage of establishing a sourdough calls for mixing flour and water. The dough is then left to rest. As it rests, it attracts the ambient yeasts in the air. Grapes, potatoes, onions, and apples contain a high percentage of the natural yeasts desirable for creating a starter. Adding small amounts of this produce to the flour and water mixture will speed the process of creating a starter. When the yeast starts to feed, grow, and reproduce in the mixture, it ferments the dough, making it bubbly and airy and giving it a tangy or sour aroma. The dough will expand to double its original volume, start to fall when the yeast activity peaks, and then begin to decline as the yeast consumes the food source.

REPLENISHING A STARTER

Left unattended, the yeast will die. To keep the starter alive, or to maintain or build up an established starter, it should be given additional feedings of flour and water. Once a starter is established, it should be replenished once or more daily until the desired amount is achieved. After it is built up, it should be replenished to maintain a par level. The starter can be replenished after it has risen and begins to fall. This is the signal that the culture has digested enough nutrients, in turn causing the collapse of the mixture. Replenishing at least three to five times is usually sufficient. The amount of replenishing can vary as long as the temperature and flour-to-water ratio is correct and is the same one used to establish the starter.

When a balanced, vigorous culture is established, it will provide leavening and flavor to bread, and the presence of organic acids from the sourdough and the higher acidity of the bread will give it a better shelf life. Another benefit of a well-balanced and well-maintained culture is that it can be maintained indefinitely.

Sourdough starters that are held under refrigeration and not used frequently must be fed at least every 3 weeks if they are to remain active.

THE BASIC STEPS TO REPLENISH A STARTER

1. *Remove the starter from refrigeration and let it rest at 75°F/24°C for 12 to 14 hours.*

2. *Feed it with a mixture of flour and water; add as much of this mixture as necessary to produce the amount of starter required for your formula. Wheat starters should be fed with a mixture of flour and water that is 66 percent hydration; for example, for every 1 lb/454 g of flour you add to the starter, add about 10½ oz/315 mL of water. Rye starters should be fed with a mixture that is at 100 percent hydration; add equal amounts of rye flour and water (by weight) to the starter. Allow the starter to ferment for 24 hours, covered and at room temperature.*

3. *Feed the starter once more on the following day at the same hydration level and allow it to ferment for 24 hours at 75°F/24°C before using it in a bread formula.*

MIXING BREAD DOUGH

In bread making, as with any baked item, the proper execution of mixing is crucial to the quality of the end product. When mixing bread dough, there are four identifiable stages that signal a change in structure and the stage of development of the dough.

STAGE 1—PICK-UP PERIOD. *During the pick-up period the ingredients are blended on low speed, until just combined. The dough is a wet, sticky, rough mass at this point.*

STAGE 2—CLEANUP PERIOD OR PRELIMINARY DEVELOPMENT. *The cleanup period is the preliminary development of the dough. At this point the dough is mixing at a moderate speed and will appear somewhat rough.*

STAGE 3—INITIAL DEVELOPMENT PERIOD. *During the initial development period, the elasticity of the gluten begins to develop and the dough starts to pull away from the sides of the mixing bowl. At this point the mixer should be running at medium speed; a high speed would work the dough too roughly, breaking the structure of the gluten rather than promoting its development.*

STAGE 4—FINAL DEVELOPMENT PERIOD. *At this point the gluten is fully developed. The dough is smooth and elastic and leaves the sides of the bowl completely clean as the mixer is running. The test for full gluten development is to check the "gluten window." To do this, remove a piece of dough from the mixer, dip it in flour, and stretch it from underneath to form a "window." If the dough is able to stretch to form a thin membrane, allowing light to filter through, then the gluten has been properly and sufficiently developed. If the dough has been undermixed, it will not have developed enough elasticity to be stretched into a thin, smooth window. If the dough is overmixed it will be very sticky and wet and will have little or no elasticity. This occurs because the gluten strands have been broken down; the resulting product will not rise or bake properly.*

The Straight Method

The straight mixing method is most often used with formulas that rely on direct fermentation. For this mixing method, the ingredients are added in a different order depending on the type of yeast used. If instant dry yeast is used, the yeast should first be blended with the flour then all the remaining ingredients should be added to the flour-yeast mixture. If active dry or compressed fresh yeast is used, the yeast should first be blended with the water and allowed to fully dissolve. Next the flour should be added and all remaining ingredients should be placed on top of the flour. After all the ingredients are in the mixing bowl, they should be blended together on low speed until just combined. Then the mixer is turned to medium speed and the dough blended to full development.

Autolyse Method

Using an autolyse when mixing bread may be used in any lean dough, and it is especially useful when making fiber-enriched dough. *Autolyse* means that the flour and water, yeast and pre-ferment are briefly combined, just enough for a rough mixture to form, and then the mixture is left to rest for 10 to 30 minutes. This allows the flour to absorb enough water for gluten development to begin. The gluten relaxes, since mixing is not agitating it. The dough has rested sufficiently when it appears very smooth.

One advantage of autolyse mixing is that mixing times are shortened, and shorter mixing times produce gluten that has greater extensibility. Another advantage is the development of a sweet aroma and flavor in the baked loaf.

The salt is added to the dough after the autolyse is complete. Added earlier, the salt would tighten the gluten. The dough is mixed until the gluten is properly developed and it is ready for bulk fermentation.

Enriched Dough

The term *enriching* indicates that ingredients containing fat or sugar are added to the dough. Many different ingredients, such as milk, oil, or butter, may be used to enrich a dough. Often, enriched breads also contain a measure of sugar that has been introduced through either the addition of ingredients that contain some type of sugar (e.g., lactose, through the use of milk), or simply by the addition of a granulated or syrup form of sugar.

The addition of fat or sugar dramatically affects the finished product. The additional fat acts to shorten the gluten strands and increase the elasticity of the gluten in a dough. This will have a tenderizing effect on the finished product, yielding a more tender crumb and the development of a soft crust. Additional sugars promote quick fermentation and browning of the crust during baking.

Fiber-Enriched Dough

Whole wheat flour and flour made from grains such as rye, barley, buckwheat, rice, oats, millet, corn, and soy all contribute distinctive tastes and textures, as well as nutrition, to breads. They also make them heavier and denser. Typically, some measure of bread flour is included in formulas calling for whole wheat or non-wheat flours in order to develop a light, open crumb.

The bran in whole-grain flours interferes with the development of gluten. Bran cuts the strands of gluten, inhibiting their development and reducing their ability to trap the carbon dioxide produced by the yeast. The higher the percentage of whole wheat or non-wheat flour in a formula, the more pronounced its effect will be on the characteristic of the finished loaf. One of the ways bread bakers aid the development of gluten in formulas containing these flours is known as *autolyse*. The flour and water are briefly combined first, just enough for a rough mixture to form, and then the dough rests to allow the gluten to relax and the dry ingredients to hydrate.

Desired Dough Temperature (DDT)

The desired dough temperature is the ideal average temperature of a dough while you are working with it. For lean doughs, this temperature is typically 75° to 80°F/24° to 27°C. Working with a lean dough at this temperature will help to keep the gluten strands relaxed. The ideal DDT for enriched doughs is slightly higher, as it is important to keep the fats that have been added to the dough soft while it is being worked.

Dough temperature is important because it directly affects fermentation. Suggested temperatures for certain ingredients are based upon the desired dough temperature (which is included in each formula). The colder the final temperature of a dough, the longer the fermentation time will be; the warmer the final dough temperature, the more quickly a dough will ferment. The fermentation time directly affects the quality and consistency of the finished product, and impacts production schedules as well, making the desired dough temperature a very important factor in bread baking.

SOAKERS

When adding a significant quantity of smaller grains, or any amount of large, whole grains such as wheat berries, it is best to soak the grains first before incorporating them into the final dough. Whole grains tend to deprive the dough of moisture and will also damage the developing gluten network.

A soaker can be made using one of two methods: hot or cold. A hot soaker pregelatinizes the starch of the soaker's grain, which can improve the crust and decrease baking time of some whole-grain breads. Hot soakers work faster, but some bakers feel that there is some loss of flavor and quality. A hot soaker is produced by bringing the liquid to a boil and then incorporating the grains. Continue to cook the mixture for about 5 minutes over low heat. Set the soaker aside for at least 1 hour or overnight to allow it to cool before adding it to the dough.

A cold soaker must be prepared at least a day in advance. For a cold soaker, the grains and liquid are incorporated slightly, covered, and allowed to soak overnight.

Soakers are added to the dough after it has started to develop and are mixed into the dough on medium speed for a few minutes to develop gluten structure, just until they are fully and evenly incorporated.

Dough with a high percentage of rye should have all the grains added at the beginning of mixing.

The temperature of a directly fermented dough immediately after mixing is influenced by three factors: the temperature of the ingredients when added, the ambient (room) temperature, and the friction created by the mixer during mixing. (For a dough produced using the indirect fermentation method, all of these factors apply, along with the temperature of all pre-ferments added to the dough.) The combination of all the factors affecting the temperature of a dough is known as the total temperature factor (TTF).

The typical desired dough temperature for most yeast doughs is 75°F/24°C; however, an acceptable temperature for a finished dough may be from 65° to 85°F/18° to 29°C.

To produce a dough within its temperature range, the temperature of the water is critical because it is the easiest factor to control with precision. It is common to use ice water when it is necessary to cool a dough. Cooling a dough by this method is useful, for example, when a long mixing time is predicted, when fermentation needs to be slowed, or when the ambient temperature is high and cannot be controlled. If pre-ferment is added that has been stored under refrigeration, it may be necessary to use slightly warm water.

Folding

Dough is folded over to redistribute the available food supply for the yeast, equalize the temperature of the dough, expel the built-up fermentation gas (carbon dioxide) and ethyl alcohol, and further develop the gluten in the dough. This may be done during bulk fermentation, bench rest, or final fermentation.

Doughs that have a typical hydration of around 67 percent or less should be treated gently during the folding process. It is more difficult for the gases resulting from the fermentation process to leaven the bread because of its density and the tightness of the gluten. For these reasons, it is important to fold carefully to preserve the already developed structure. A slack (wet) dough, such as that for ciabatta, requires more aggressive treatment when folding over. It is more difficult to develop the gluten in slack doughs; they require more gluten development to hold their shape and retain their inner structure.

Scaling and Preshaping

Accurate scaling guarantees the correct weight of the dough pieces when dividing. However, scaling should be done quickly, so as not to over-age the dough. Scaling time should not exceed 15 to 20 minutes. Proper scaling will also allow for uniformity in proofing and baking times. Dough is usually divided either entirely by hand using a scale, or first divided into large portions by hand and then divided into smaller pieces with a dough divider.

After scaling, the dough is given a gentle first shaping or "preshaping." Always lay the shaped pieces on the bench in the order they are shaped, in regular rows, so that you can start with the first piece when giving the dough the final shaping. The objective of preshaping is to get a smooth, tight skin that will help to trap the gases that develop during fermentation.

During scaling and preshaping, two things happen to the dough: First, because it is cut, the carbon dioxide trapped inside begins to escape, which causes the structure of the dough to begin to collapse; and second, the gluten strands are worked, which causes them to contract, making the dough tighter and tougher to work with.

THE BASIC STEPS FOR PRESHAPING LARGE ROUNDS (FROM 6 OZ TO 4½ LB/170 G TO 2.04 KG)

1. *Position the dough so one long edge is parallel to the edge of the work surface.*

2. *Fold the top edge of the dough down to the bottom edge. Using the heel of your hand, seal the two edges together. Rotate the dough 90 degrees.*

3. *Fold the top edge of the dough down to the bottom edge. Using the heel of your hand, seal the two edges together. Place the seam on bottom.*

4. *Cup both hands around the dough and pull it toward you, giving it a one-quarter turn; continue until fully tightened.*

THE BASIC STEPS FOR PRESHAPING SMALL ROUNDS (FROM 2 TO 6 OZ/57 TO 170 G)

1. *Position the dough so one long edge is parallel to the edge of the work surface.*

2. *Fold the top edge of the dough down to the bottom edge. Using the heel of your hand, seal the two edges together. Rotate the dough 90 degrees.*

3. *Fold the top edge of the dough down to the bottom edge. Using the heel of your hand, seal the two edges together.*

4. Place your hand over the ball of dough and curl your fingers so that the first knuckles of your fingers are touching the table. Your fingertips should almost be touching the palm of your hand, and your thumb should be out to the side and touching the table; the heel of your hand should also be touching the table. The dough should be sitting near the top of your palm, near your thumb, forefinger, and middle finger.

5. Using your palm, push the dough away from you in an arc to the right. Using your fingertips, pull the dough toward you in an arc to the left. Repeat this circular motion, applying gentle pressure while rounding the dough, to create a tight, smooth ball.

THE BASIC STEPS FOR PRESHAPING LARGE OBLONGS (FROM 12 OZ TO 1¾ LB/340 TO 794 G)

1. Position the dough so one long edge is parallel to the edge of the work surface.

2. Stretch the dough into a rectangle 10 in/25 cm long. Fold the left and right edges of the rectangle into the center of the dough, pressing the dough lightly with your fingertips.

3. Fold the top edge of the dough down to the center of the dough, pressing lightly with your fingertips. Fold the top of the dough down to the bottom edge. Seal the two edges together, using the heel of your hand.

4. Roll the dough into an even cylinder 6 in/15 cm long.

THE BASIC STEPS FOR PRESHAPING SMALL OBLONGS (FROM 3 TO 6 OZ/85 TO 170 G)

1. Turn the dough so one long edge is parallel to the edge of the work surface.

2. Stretch the dough into a rectangle 3 in/8 cm long. Fold the left and right edges of the rectangle into the center of the dough, pressing the dough lightly with your fingertips.

3. Fold the top edge of the dough down to the center of the dough, pressing lightly with your fingertips. Fold the top of the dough down to the bottom edge. Seal the two edges together, using the heel of your hand.

4. Roll the dough into an even cylinder 3 in/7.5 cm long.

Resting or Intermediate Fermentation

The intermediate fermentation or resting stage allows the dough to relax and recover from being divided and preshaped before the final shaping. Intermediate fermentation allows the gluten to relax, so the dough will become somewhat slack and easier to manipulate into its final shape, and it allows the yeast cells to recover, rebuilding carbon dioxide and therefore the internal structure of the dough. Normally, this stage lasts from 10 to 20 minutes. It is important to keep the loaves covered with plastic wrap or a moist linen cloth to prevent the formation of a skin or dry crust.

Final Shaping

After the secondary fermentation, the dough is given its final shape. Following are two of the most basic and common shaping techniques: the *boule* and the *bâtard*. Brush the dough with egg wash or water, if using, after it is shaped so that the dough can be evenly coated without affecting it after its final rise. Any simple garnishes such as seeds or coarse salt can be applied once the surface is brushed with egg wash or water; the wash will hold them in place.

The Basic Steps for Shaping a Boule

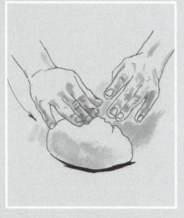 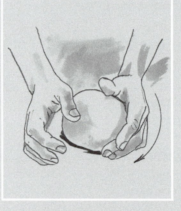 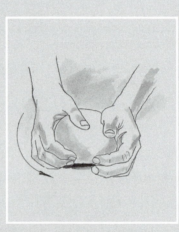

1 *Preshape the dough into a round and allow to rest, uncovered, until relaxed, 15 to 20 minutes.*

2 *Cup both hands around the dough. Using your thumbs, push the dough away from you in an arc to the right.*

3 *Using the edges of your palms as a guide, pull the dough toward you in an arc to the left.*

The Basic Steps for Shaping a Batard

1 *Gently flatten the preshaped oblong.*

2 *Fold the top of the dough to the center.*

3 *Press the seam with your fingertips to tighten the dough.*

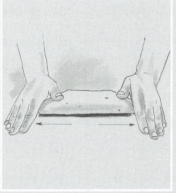

4 *Roll the ends of the cylinder with the palms of your hands to taper.*

Final Fermentation (Proofing)

After shaping, the dough undergoes one more fermentation either on a worktable or sheet pans, or in bread baskets or molds; these are usually dusted with flour or cornmeal. During this final rise, it is again important to ensure that a skin does not form on the surface of the dough. If you are not using a proof box for this final proof, the dough should be covered. Using the temperature and humidity controls in a proof box will prevent a skin from forming without the dough being covered.

A temperature and humidity controlled proof box can provide the necessary relative humidity of approximately 80 percent, so the surface of the dough does not dry out. (Conversely, if the humidity is too high, the loaves will become too sticky for proper crust formation.) The ambient temperature for the final proof should be between 80° and 90°F/27° and 32°C for maximum yeast activity; the ideal temperature is 85°F/29°C. If the temperature during this final proof is too high, insufficient yeast activity will result in poor grain and loss of flavor, and the shelf life of the bread will be shorter. A temperature that is too low will result in a longer proofing time.

BREAD FINISHING TECHNIQUES

Scoring and washes, when used, enhance the overall beauty of the finished loaf or roll. Scoring allows for full expansion, as well as controlling the final expansion, so the loaf does not become misshapen. Washes control the crust development during baking.

Scoring

Many breads are scored with a razor, sharp knife, or scissors before they are loaded into the oven. Scoring helps develop a good-quality loaf with an even appearance and crumb. It allows the bread to release steam and continue to expand until the structure is set. By scoring the dough, the baker can control the final shape of the bread by controlling where the product expands during baking. Baking an unscored bread results in an unevenly shaped loaf. The structure forms too early to permit full expansion and, consequently, the full development of the internal structure of the loaf.

Some breads, such as baguettes, are scored with traditional patterns that are used as a way to label the breads, making it easy for both clients and staff to identify them.

Scoring

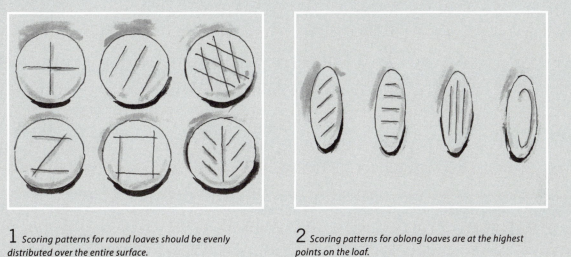

1 *Scoring patterns for round loaves should be evenly distributed over the entire surface.*

2 *Scoring patterns for oblong loaves are at the highest points on the loaf.*

Washes

Water is often brushed or sprayed on shaped breads before baking to ensure a crisp crust and to promote the gelatinization of the starch on the surface of the bread. A wash of beaten eggs creates a glossy, shiny crust and seals in the moisture of the bread. Typically, whole eggs are used. A wash of only yolks would burn more quickly, especially at the higher temperatures required for baking most breads.

Milk or cream is often used as a wash for breads baked at lower temperatures. Because the lactose in milk (or cream) caramelizes at 170°F/77°C, it gives breads a darker crust than water. In addition, the bread will bake a little faster because the milk fat acts to conduct heat.

CLOCKWISE FROM TOP:
Pullman pan, peel, bench
brush, standard loaf pan,
mini loaf pans, bench
knife, lame, oblong
dough-rising basket with
liner, round dough-rising
basket with liner, couche
(on bottom), and round
dough-rising basket.

TOOLS FOR BREAD BAKING

Some breads require special equipment for shaping, fermenting, and/or baking. A wide variety of dough-rising baskets, liners, and baking pans are available to accommodate loaves of many sizes and shapes.

Lame

Lame is the French word for "razor," and it is a tool used by bakers to slash loaves right before baking. The extra-sharp, curved razor blade clamped into a stainless-steel, wooden, or plastic handle cuts just under the surface of the dough, allowing room for expansion during baking. Making these cuts, scores, or ears allows the baker to control how and where the bread expansion will occur.

Patterns and designs can be created in proofed yeast breads and rolls using a lame. The scoring should be evenly distributed over the surface of the loaf, and cuts should be made higher up on oblong loaves. A very sharp edge is needed to cut the dough cleanly without tearing or pulling. The cutting motion should be swift, deliberate, and at an angle.

Oven Peels

Peels are large, flat wooden paddles designed for transferring doughs onto the deck of an oven. To use a peel, sprinkle it with cornmeal before loading the dough onto it. Use a quick jerking motion to slide the dough off the peel onto the deck of the oven.

Bench Knife

A bench knife has a thin, stiff rectangular steel blade set in a wooden or plastic handle to make it easier to grip and use. The blade, which is usually 6 in/15 cm wide, has no sharpened edges, making it useful for scraping, lifting, folding, and cutting dough.

Couche

Freestanding breads like baguettes, ciabatta, and rolls need some support during the proofing process. The *couche,* French for "resting place," is a heavy linen or canvas cloth that is floured and pleated to hold several loaves. The folds and rough fabric help the dough keep its shape and absorb excess moisture, giving the bread a crisp crust.

Shape the dough into the desired shape, place the loaf onto the couche, and lift the fabric up to create walls between the loaves. These walls will prevent sticking and will hold the loaves. Once they have risen, roll the loaves onto a peel, then roll into the oven. Shake excess flour off the couche when done. Hang in a dry area and do not wash.

Dough-Rising Baskets

Also called *brotformen* or *bannetons,* dough-rising baskets are round or oblong straw or willow baskets used for proofing, molding, and shaping bread. Some are lined with linen.

Durum Pizza Dough

MAKES 15 LB 11¾ OZ/7.12 KG DOUGH (ABOUT 27 PIZZA
CRUSTS). DDT: 75°F/24°C.

INGREDIENT	U.S.	METRIC
Bread flour	5 lb 5 oz	2.41 kg
Durum flour	3 lb 14 oz	1.76 kg
Instant dry yeast	¾ oz	21 g
Water	94 fl oz	2.82 L
Olive oil	5½ oz	156 g
Salt	4 oz	113 g

1. Combine the flours and yeast. Add the water, olive oil, and salt to the mixer and then add the flour and yeast. Mix on low speed with the dough hook attachment for 4 minutes and then on medium speed for 4 minutes. The dough should have good gluten development but still be a little sticky. Mix until full gluten development is achieved.

2. Bulk ferment the dough until nearly doubled, about 30 minutes. Fold gently.

3. Divide the dough into 9-oz/255-g pieces. Preshape the dough into large rounds. Let the dough rest, covered, under refrigeration overnight. Remove from the refrigerator 1 hour before use.

4. Using a rolling pin, roll each piece of dough into a 9-in/23-cm round. Transfer the rounds to a peel that has been dusted with semolina flour before topping.

5. Top the dough as desired, leaving a 1-in/2.5-cm border to brush with olive oil.

6. Load the pizzas into a 475°F/246°C deck oven and bake until golden brown around the edges, 8 to 12 minutes. Serve at once.

Use a peel to place the pizza into the oven and remove it after baking.

QUICK BREADS

Quick breads are served as simple desserts or as breakfast pastries. When preparing quick breads, it is important to sift the dry ingredients together both to remove lumps and to blend the dry ingredients evenly, which will in turn help to ensure a fully combined batter with minimal mixing time. A short mixing time is an important factor because, unlike yeast-raised breads, gluten development is undesirable in quick breads.

The Blending Method

Most quick breads are prepared using the blending method. (A few quick breads are prepared using the creaming method. See page 76 for information on the creaming method.) The blending method consists of making two mixtures, one with the wet ingredients and one with the dry, then combining the two together.

THE BASIC STEPS OF THE BLENDING METHOD

1. *Sift the flour with the other dry ingredients. All-purpose or pastry flour is used for most items made by this method because of its moderate protein content. Special flours such as cornmeal or whole wheat flour may replace some or all of the white wheat flour in a given formula to add flavor and develop a different texture. The flour(s) should be sifted together with the other dry ingredients, such as baking soda, baking powder, sugar, salt, cocoa, or ground spices. It is important to sift the dry ingredients, as sifting removes lumps and incorporates all ingredients together. Thoroughly blending the dry ingredients also ensures that the leavening agent will be evenly distributed in the mixture. Sifting will ultimately help to create a fully combined batter needing minimal mixing time.*

2. *Combine the wet ingredients. Cream, milk, buttermilk, water, and even watery vegetables like zucchini all add moisture to a baking formula. Fats shorten developing gluten strands, which helps to create a tender texture in the baked good. Solid fats like butter or shortening are most often melted for this method so they can be blended with the other liquid ingredients. All ingredients should be at room temperature before being added, as those that are too cold may cause the batter to separate.*

3. *Add all the wet ingredients to the dry ingredients all at once and blend, using a mixer or by hand, just until the dry ingredients are evenly moistened. Mixing these batters as briefly as possible ensures a light, delicate texture. Overmixed batters may develop too much gluten and the resulting item will not have the desired fine, delicate texture.*

4. *Scrape the bowl down once or twice to mix the batter evenly.*

TOOLS FOR MAKING QUICK BREADS

One advantage of quick breads is that their preparation does not require any specialty tools; however, quick bread batter must be baked in a pan. Quick breads are most often baked in standard size or mini loaf pans, but round or rectangular baking pans or muffin pans may also be used.

Brioche Loaf

MAKES 11 LB 10¾ OZ/5.29 KG DOUGH. DDT: 75°F/24°C

INGREDIENT	U.S.	METRIC
Bread flour	5 lb	2.27 kg
Instant dry yeast	1¼ oz	35 g
Eggs	2 lb	907 g
Milk, at room temperature	16 fl oz	480 mL
Sugar	8 oz	227 g
Salt	1½ oz	43 g
Butter, soft but still pliable	3 lb	1.36 kg
Egg wash	as needed	

1. Combine the flour and yeast in a bowl. Place the eggs, milk, sugar, and salt in the mixer and then add the flour and yeast. Mix on low speed with the dough hook attachment for 4 minutes.

2. Gradually add the butter with the mixer running on medium speed, scraping down the sides of the bowl as necessary. After the butter has been fully incorporated, mix on medium speed for 15 minutes, or until the dough begins to pull away from the sides of the bowl.

3. Line a sheet pan with parchment paper and grease the paper. Place the dough on the sheet pan. Cover tightly with plastic wrap and refrigerate overnight.

4. Lightly grease ten to twelve 2-lb/907-g loaf pans (4½ in/11 cm wide, 8 in/20 cm long, and 3 in/8 cm deep).

5. Remove the dough from the refrigerator and divide it by hand into 2-oz/57-g pieces. Preshape each piece into a round, lightly flouring the work surface as needed. (Reminder: Refrigerate the dough as necessary during shaping to keep it cool and workable.) Refrigerate the rolls until cool, about 15 minutes.

6. Place the pieces of dough in the loaf pans in two rows of four. Brush lightly with egg wash, brushing away any excess that accumulates in the crevices. Proof, covered, until the dough is almost double in size and springs back slowly to the touch but does not collapse, 1 to 2 hours.

7. Gently brush the dough again with egg wash. Bake in a 375°F/191°C deck oven until the crust is a rich golden brown and the sides of the bread spring back fully when pressed, 30 to 35 minutes. Remove from the pans and cool completely on racks.

Loaf Pans

Loaf pans, or tins, are oblong or rectangular pans used to bake pound cakes, other loaf cakes, and quick breads, as well as loaves of yeast-raised bread. They are made of glass or metal, with or without a nonstick coating. They are available in a wide range of sizes from large to mini. A pullman loaf pan has a sliding cover and is used to prepare perfectly square finely grained slicing loaves (also known as *pain de mie*). The pans are typically made of tinned steel. A pan for a 1½-lb/680-g loaf is 4¼ in/10.60 cm wide by 13 in/33 cm long by 4 in/10 cm deep, and a pan for a 2-lb/907-g loaf is 4 by 16 by 4 in/10 by 41 by 10 cm.

Gently place the dough into loaf pans for baking.

Banana Bread

YIELD: 6 LOAVES (1 LB 14 OZ/851 G EACH)

INGREDIENT	U.S.	METRIC
All-purpose flour	2 lb 13 oz	1.30 kg
Baking powder	2½ tsp	7.50 g
Baking soda	¾ oz	20 g
Salt	1½ tsp	7.50 g
Bananas, very ripe	4 lb 4 oz	1.90 kg
Lemon juice	1 tbsp	15 mL
Sugar	2 lb 13 oz	1.30 kg
Eggs	12 oz	340 g
Vegetable oil	14 oz	400 g
Pecans, coarsely chopped and toasted	8 oz	230 g

1. Preheat the oven to 350°F/175°C.

2. Coat the loaf pans with a light film of fat.

3. Sift together the flour, baking powder, baking soda, and salt.

4. Purée the bananas with the lemon juice until creamy and smooth.

5. In the bowl of a stand mixer, combine the banana purée, sugar, eggs, and oil and mix on medium speed with the paddle attachment until blended. Scrape down the bowl as needed..

6. Add the sifted dry ingredients on low speed and mix until just combined. Scrape down the bowl as needed. Remove the bowl from the mixer and stir in the pecans.

7. Scale 1 lb 14 oz/851 g batter into each prepared pan. Gently tap the filled pans to burst any large air bubbles.

8. Bake until the bread springs back when pressed and a tester inserted near the center comes out clean, about 55 minutes.

9. Cool the loaves in the pans for a few minutes, then unmold onto racks and cool completely.

PASTRY, CAKE, AND COOKIE TOOLS AND TECHNIQUES

Pastries, cakes, and cookies are all made of the same basic ingredients, but different preparation techniques give them vastly different characteristics that are featured in a

These foundational preparations may be served as stand-alone desserts, assembled into classical or contemporary cakes and tortes, or used as components in complex plated

MIXING METHODS

Even though most doughs and batters contain flour, fat, liquid, and eggs, what makes each product different is the method for mixing or combining these common ingredients.

The Creaming Method

Muffins, cake, quick breads, cookies, and other baked goods made with the creaming method develop their light and airy structure through the incorporation of air during mixing and by the use of chemical leaveners. For the creaming method, first the fat and sugar are "creamed," or blended until very smooth and light. Then the eggs are added, and finally the sifted dry ingredients are added in two or three additions; if there is any liquid, the dry ingredients and liquid are added alternately, starting and ending with the dry ingredients. It is important that ingredients for a creamed batter or dough are at room temperature and the fat (butter, shortening, nut paste, etc.) is soft before beginning to mix.

THE BASIC STEPS OF THE CREAMING MIXING METHOD

1. *Cream together the fat and sugar on medium speed with the paddle attachment, scraping down the sides and bottom of the bowl occasionally as you work to ensure all the fat is blended evenly. Cream the fat and sugar until the mixture is pale in color and light and smooth in texture; when the butter and sugar have this appearance, it indicates that a sufficient amount of air has been incorporated into the mixture. If the ingredients are not sufficiently creamed, the final product will be dense and lack the light, tender qualities characteristic of creamed baked goods. However, there are formulas made by the* creaming method, such as some cookies, where minimum air incorporation is desirable. In these cases the butter and sugar are blended for a shorter amount of time, just until the mixture is smooth.

2. *Once the butter and the sugar are properly creamed, the eggs should be added gradually and in stages, mixing the batter until fully incorporated and scraping down the bowl after each addition. Scraping down the bowl is important to develop a completely smooth batter. Adding the eggs in batches will help to prevent the batter from separating. Blending eggs into the butter-sugar mixture creates an emulsion. The more eggs added, the more difficult it becomes to sustain the emulsion, and the mixture can begin to separate, developing a curdled or broken appearance. Using eggs at room temperature, or warming the eggs slightly (not above 80°F/27°C) when an unusually large amount is to be added, will help to emulsify and fully blend the mixture. If the mixture should separate, continue to mix until it becomes smooth again. However, sometimes this curdled appearance is unavoidable because of the ratio of eggs to fat. In these instances, blend in the eggs to create as smooth a mixture as possible, and when the dry ingredients are added make sure to blend to a smooth consistency.*

3. *The sifted dry ingredients are generally added in one of two ways: all at once, or alternating with the liquid ingredient (milk, juice, etc.). When adding the dry and liquid ingredients alternately, add one-third of the dry ingredients, then about one-half of the liquid ingredients, mixing until smooth and scraping down the bowl after each addition. Repeat this sequence until all of the dry and liquid ingredients have been added, ending with the dry ingredients. Increase the speed and beat the batter just until it is evenly blended and smooth. Sometimes, but not often, the liquid may*

be added to the creamed mixture immediately after the eggs. This is done only when the amount of liquid is very small, as a large amount of liquid is likely to cause the creamed mixture to separate. It is difficult to get a creamed mixture to accept a large amount liquid. Regardless of the method of addition, after adding the dry ingredients, mix the dough or batter minimally, or just until incorporated. Excessive mixing would act to develop gluten, which would toughen the dough or batter and, therefore, the final product.

4. Add any remaining flavoring or garnishing ingredients, mixing or folding until they are just incorporated.

The Two-Stage Method

This mixing method is used when making high-ratio cakes. With a higher proportion of sugar and emulsifiers than other cakes, a high-ratio cake is one in which the weight of the sugar is equal to or greater than the weight of the flour, and the weight of the eggs is equal to or greater than the weight of the fat. The high ratio of eggs to shortening acts as an emulsifier. When added to the dry and liquid ingredients, this emulsion helps to create a smooth batter.

THE BASIC STEPS OF THE TWO-STAGE MIXING METHOD

1. Combine or sift together all of the dry ingredients.

2. Combine all of the wet ingredients, including the eggs.

3. In the first stage of mixing, combine the dry ingredient mixture with all of the fat and half of the liquid mixture in the bowl of an electric mixer fitted with the paddle attachment. Mix for 4 minutes on medium speed, scraping down the bowl periodically to ensure the batter is mixed evenly.

4. In the second stage, blend the remaining liquid into the batter in three equal parts, mixing for 2 minutes after each addition, for a total of 6 minutes. Scrape down the bowl periodically to make certain that the batter is blended evenly. The development of flavor and texture in a product created using the two-stage mixing method can be attributed to the specific and longer mixing times as compared to others.

The Angel Food Method

Angel food is a light, spongy cake based on beaten egg whites and sugar (a meringue) that is stabilized with flour. All of the leavening in an angel food cake is supplied by the air that is whipped into the meringue. It is drier than sponge or chiffon cakes because it does not contain any fat. These cakes have good structure, but because they contain no fat, they have a unique texture, which makes them less desirable for use in layer cakes or as a component of any layered, sliced dessert or pastry.

THE BASIC STEPS OF THE ANGEL FOOD MIXING METHOD

1. Assemble all equipment and ingredients and sift the flour before beginning to mix. This is important because thorough preparation will ensure the batter goes from the mixer to the oven in the shortest amount of time; the less time the batter stands in the mixer the less volume will be lost in the batter, resulting in a cake with maximum volume.

2. Whip the egg whites on high speed using the whisk attachment until they form soft peaks. Continue whipping and add the sugar, streaming it in gradually with the machine running. All of the leavening in an angel food cake is supplied by the air that is whipped into the meringue.

Eggs lend stability to a product when baking. They also have leavening power; egg whites especially, as they are whipped, trap air, which expands when heated. This ultimately creates a larger and lighter product as demonstrated in angel food cake's characteristically spongy and airy texture. When sugar is added in the whipping process, the combination of the eggs' moisture along with the mixing agitation causes the sugar to begin dissolving; the sugar in turn coats the air bubbles in the eggs, making them more stable.

3. *Once the meringue has medium, glossy peaks, fold in the sifted dry ingredients by hand, working quickly to reduce the deflation of the beaten egg whites.*

   Flour acts as perhaps the most common stabilizer in baking; its gluten content (the protein component) builds structure and strength in baked goods. It is important that the flour is sifted, as sifting introduces air into the mixture, as well as preventing an uneven, lumpy texture.

4. *Sprinkle the tube pan with a small amount of water before adding the batter to help develop a thin crisp crust on the cake.*

Cold and Warm Foaming Methods

A foaming method is any method in which eggs are whipped or beaten to incorporate air before they are mixed into a batter. The air incorporated into the eggs creates a light and airy batter as well and helps to leaven the final baked item. The air trapped in the eggs will form pockets that, during baking, will expand and cause the product to rise.

When using a foaming method, it is important that all ingredients and equipment be assembled and receive any preliminary treatment before beginning

to mix the ingredients; this will help to ensure that the foaming process proceeds as quickly as possible, thus preventing any loss of volume in the batter.

Flour and any other dry ingredients should be sifted thoroughly to ensure full aeration.

Butter should be melted and allowed to cool slightly.

THE BASIC STEPS OF THE COLD FOAMING METHOD

1. *Place the eggs and sugar in the bowl of a mixer large enough to accommodate the volume of the fully beaten eggs.*

2. *Using the wire whisk attachment, whip the mixture to maximum volume on high speed.*

   Remove the bowl from the mixer. To determine when the eggs have reached maximum volume, watch as they are beaten; when the aerated mixture just begins to recede, maximum volume has been achieved. They will typically expand 4 to 6 times their original volume.

3. *Fold the sifted dry ingredients into the beaten eggs gently and gradually, but quickly, to prevent excessive loss of volume. For folding, use a large rubber spatula or other implement with a large, broad, flat surface. This will allow for a larger amount of batter to be lifted with each fold, facilitating the rapid incorporation of ingredients without breaking down the fragile aerated structure.*

4. *Fold the melted fat into the batter last. You may want to temper in the butter; some chefs feel this eases the fat's full incorporation and lessens any deflating effects on the batter. To do this, first lighten the butter by incorporating a small amount of batter. Then fold this mixture into the remaining batter.*

5. *Immediately after mixing, scale the batter into each prepared pan and bake.*

THE BASIC STEPS OF THE WARM FOAMING METHOD

1. *Place the eggs and sugar in the bowl of a mixer and place the bowl over a pan of barely simmering water. Stir the mixture with a wire whisk until it reaches 110°F/43°C. Heating the eggs with the sugar before beating allows the mixture to achieve maximum volume faster and creates a more stable foam because the sugar has been dissolved and the protein in the eggs has become more elastic.*

2. *Using the wire whisk attachment, whip the mixture to maximum volume on high speed.*

3. *After the egg mixture has reached maximum volume, reduce the mixer speed to medium and continue to blend for 5 additional minutes. Whipping at high speed creates large air bubbles; continuing to mix at a lower speed divides the bubbles, reducing their size and creating a more stable foam, thereby stabilizing the batter.*

4. *Fold the sifted dry ingredients into the beaten eggs gently and gradually, but quickly, to prevent excessive loss of volume. For folding, use a large rubber spatula or other implement with a large, broad, flat surface. This will allow for a larger amount of batter to be lifted with each fold, facilitating the rapid incorporation of ingredients without breaking down the fragile aerated structure.*

5. *Fold the melted fat into the batter last. You may want to temper in the butter; some chefs feel this eases the fat's full incorporation and lessens any deflating effects on the batter. To do this, first lighten the butter by incorporating a small amount of batter. Then fold this mixture into the remaining batter.*

6. *Immediately after mixing, scale the batter into each prepared pan and bake.*

The Separated Foaming Method

In this variation on a standard cold foam mixing method, the whole eggs are separated and beaten separately into two foams. These foams are then folded together. The separated foam mixing method is slightly more difficult than the cold foaming method because the egg whites, which are whipped alone, can rapidly lose volume. For this reason it is important that all ingredients and equipment are assembled and receive any preliminary treatment before you begin to mix the batter (e.g., pans are lined, dry ingredients are sifted, fat is melted, etc.). Dry ingredients should be sifted for aeration as well as to preventatively smooth any lumps that may require extra mixing as they are incorporated into the delicate aerated egg mixture.

THE BASIC STEPS OF THE SEPARATED FOAMING MIXING METHOD

1. *Separate the egg whites from the egg yolks.*

2. *Whip the egg yolks with a portion of the sugar on high speed using the whisk attachment to the ribbon stage, or until the mixture has thickened enough to fall in ribbons from the whisk and is pale yellow in color. Set this foam aside. Whipped egg yolks are stable and won't lose volume.*

3. *Whip the whites, in a grease-free bowl and using a clean whisk, until soft peaks form. Gradually add the remaining sugar with the mixer running on medium speed, and continue whipping on medium or high speed until the whites form medium peaks. The point to which the whites are beaten is important. If the whites are beaten to stiff peaks, the additional agitation they undergo during folding will cause them to become overbeaten. Overbeaten eggs are less elastic, are more difficult to incorporate, break down more easily, do not develop a stable internal structure, and have less leavening power.*

4. *Immediately after the egg whites reach their desired peak, gently fold them into the foamed egg yolks. To fully blend these two components, first combine a small measure of the whites with the yolks to lighten them and make their consistency more akin to that of the whites. Fold the remaining whites into the yolk mixture.*

   Bringing the consistency of the yolks closer to that of the whites is a step taken to facilitate the quickest incorporation of the whites into the mixture. The more quickly the two egg mixtures are incorporated, the less volume is lost.

5. *Fold the sifted dry ingredients into the egg mixture gently and gradually, but quickly, to prevent excessive loss of volume. For folding, use a large rubber spatula or other implement with a large, broad, flat surface to allow for a larger amount of batter to be lifted with each fold, facilitating the rapid incorporation of ingredients without breaking down the fragile aerated structure.*

6. *Fold the melted fat into the batter last.*

7. *Immediately after mixing, scale the batter into each prepared pan and bake. The batter should be scaled into pans and baked immediately to prevent any loss of volume in the batter as it stands.*

The Combination Method

The combination mixing method combines the creaming mixing method with the foaming method. This combination gives the cake qualities of both methods: the rich, moist crumb of a creamed cake as well as some of the lightness of a batter that has the additional leavening power of beaten egg whites.

THE BASIC STEPS OF THE COMBINATION MIXING METHOD

1. *Prepare the pan(s), assemble ingredients, and sift dry ingredients. When making anything using this method, as with other foamed batters, advance preparation (pan preparation, sifting, ingredients assembly, etc.) is critical to successful completion. Advance preparation is necessary to ensure that the mixing process proceeds quickly and smoothly; this will result in a batter able to maintain maximum volume before baking.*

2. *Cream together the butter and some of the sugar. This step helps to develop air cells, which will facilitate the leavening process during baking. Evenly creamed butter and sugar will have a pale color and a light and smooth texture.*

3. *Blend the whole eggs and yolks into the creamed mixture.*

4. *Whip the egg whites on high speed using the whisk attachment until soft peaks form, and then stream in the sugar gradually with the mixer running on medium speed. Beat the egg whites until medium peaks form.*

Beaten egg whites add significant additional leavening power to the final product. The point to which they are beaten is important; if whites are beaten to stiff rather than medium peaks, the additional agitation they receive during folding will cause them to be overbeaten. Overbeaten egg whites are less elastic and harder to incorporate, break down more easily, do not develop a stable internal structure, and have less leavening power.

5. *To incorporate the egg whites into the creamed mixture while keeping as much volume as possible, first add about one-third of the beaten egg whites, blending them in gently but thoroughly, to lighten the creamed mixture. After that, the batter will accept the remaining egg whites more easily and with less vigorous mixing, allowing for less loss of volume.*

   Gentle folding prevents the whites from being overworked and aids in preserving the volume created by the air pockets in both the existing meringue as well as in the creamed mixture.

6. *Gently fold in the remaining egg whites just until evenly blended.*

7. *Fold in the sifted ingredients and any garnishes quickly but gently. The dry ingredients are added last because if they were added to the creamed mixture before the meringue, the batter would be much too stiff to accept the light, airy meringue.*

8. *Immediately after mixing, scale the batter evenly into each prepared pan and bake.*

The Chiffon Method

The chiffon mixing method is simple to execute and produces a beautiful cake with a tender, moist crumb and ample structure and stability, making it a good choice for building tiered cakes. All advance preparation (pan preparation, etc.) is important for chiffon cakes, as it is for other foamed cakes; however, it is less critical here as batters made by the chiffon mixing method are more stable than batters in which beaten (foamed) egg whites are used.

THE BASIC STEPS OF THE CHIFFON MIXING METHOD

1. *Sift together the dry ingredients and mix in a portion of the sugar.*

2. *Blend all of the wet ingredients together except for the egg whites. Next, blend the wet ingredients into the sifted dry ingredients.*

3. *Whip the egg whites on high speed using the whisk attachment until soft peaks form, then stream in the remaining sugar gradually with the mixer running on medium speed. Continue beating the egg whites until medium peaks form.*

4. *Finally, fold the meringue into the batter. To do this, first lighten the batter by incorporating approximately one-third of the egg whites. Then gently fold in the remaining two-thirds of the beaten egg whites.*

TYPES OF DOUGH

The preparation of the dough ultimately determines the texture of a baked product. For instance, a crumbly shortbread cookie has a very different texture than an airy croissant or a flaky biscuit. This is because these products are all made from different types of dough that are prepared using very dissimilar methods.

Rubbed Dough

The characteristic texture of rubbed dough is developed by rubbing together the fat and the flour, leaving flakes of fat visible.

There are two basic types of rubbed dough: flaky and mealy. The larger the flakes of fat are before the liquid is added, the flakier and crisper the baked crust will be. If the flakes of butter or shortening are rubbed into the dough just until they are about the size of peas, the dough will be what is often referred to as flaky pie dough. When the liquid is added, the dough is worked just enough to allow the moisture to be absorbed by the flour and just until the ingredients come together, at which point the dough should be allowed to rest and cool under refrigeration.

Flaky pie dough is best for pies, tarts, and other preparations where the filling is baked in the crust. It is not well suited for preparations where the crust is completely prebaked and allowed to cool before a liquid filling is added that must set under refrigeration. After baking, the pockets that lend the flaky texture to this type of dough easily allow juices or liquids to leak into the crust.

If the butter or shortening is more thoroughly worked into the dough until the mixture resembles coarse meal, the result will be what is sometimes referred to as a mealy dough. Mealy pie dough has a finer, more tender texture than does flaky pie dough. With the fat more evenly interspersed in the flour, its ability to shorten gluten strands present in the dough becomes more apparent, so the resulting dough is very tender. As with flaky pastry dough, mealy dough should be wrapped in plastic wrap and allowed to rest under refrigeration so the butter or other fat will firm and the gluten will relax before the dough is worked and rolled.

Mealy doughs are well suited for all types of pies and tarts, but most particularly for formulas that require a fully baked shell filled with a precooked filling, such as a cream, that will have to set under refrigeration before it can be sliced and served. They are also best for custard pies and for creating decorative tops such as lattice.

THE BASIC STEPS FOR MAKING RUBBED DOUGH

1. *Combine the dry ingredients. Pastry and all-purpose flours are, in general, ideal for the rubbed dough method. Cake flour is too high in starch, so it will not absorb enough water and will produce a dough with a pasty consistency. Bread flour, because of its high protein content, will absorb water quickly and in comparatively great quantities, developing gluten readily and in great amounts. This will make a dough that is tough and elastic. On the other hand, pastry flour and all-purpose flour have the proper balance of starch and protein, with the desired amount of water absorption and gluten development to produce a dough that is both flaky and tender.*

2. *Flake the firm fat into the flour. Fat contributes to the development of a flaky texture in pastry dough. The amount of fat and the way it is added to the other ingredients in a formula have significant impact on the finished baked good. Leaving the fat in pieces or chunks, rather than combining it thoroughly,*

gives dough a flaky texture. When a rubbed dough is baked, the pieces of fat melt to create pockets in the interior of the dough. As the fat melts, steam is released from the moisture held in the fat. This steam expands the pockets, which then become set as the dough continues to bake, thus creating a flaky, textured baked good. The larger the flakes of fat left in the dough, the flakier the baked dough will be.

When butter or shortening is more thoroughly incorporated into the dough, resulting in a coarse meal rather than large flakes, the resulting baked dough becomes less flaky but more tender, as the even distribution of fat serves to shorten structure-providing gluten strands in the flour as it bakes.

Butter, lard, hydrogenated shortening, and other fats may be used in the production of rubbed doughs. All of these fats are solid at room temperature, and when cold have a firm consistency that makes it possible to use them for this method. Of all the fats, butter alone will yield the most flavor, but it is difficult to handle because it has a lower melting point than shortening and lard.

3. Add all of the liquid at once to the flour-fat mixture and blend the dough quickly but thoroughly. Water is the most common liquid in rubbed dough formulas, but milk or cream may also be used. When substituting milk or cream for water in a rubbed dough formula, decrease the amount of fat to adjust for the fat present in the milk or cream.

4. Turn out the dough onto a lightly floured work surface.

5. Gather and press it together into a disk or a flat rectangle.

6. Wrap the dough tightly in plastic wrap and chill it under refrigeration until firm enough to work with. The period of rest and cooling before working and rolling is vital to ensure that the fat does not become too soft nor the flour overworked. Soft fat prevents the separation of the baked dough into layers, and overworked flour can result in a tough, rather than tender, final baked good.

7. Always keep rubbed doughs cool during mixing and when working with them. The ideal working temperature is 60°F/16°C. If the dough becomes too warm, the fat may become too soft and be absorbed into the dough, destroying the layers in the dough.

Short Dough

Short dough contains a high percentage of fat which produces a very tender and crumbly crust. If worked excessively, however, a short dough will become tough. Cake flour is the preferred choice for short dough because of its ability to absorb moisture. Short dough includes eggs, either whole eggs or yolks, and sometimes sugar, both of which contribute to the flavor and color of the dough, as well as to its tender texture.

THE BASIC STEPS FOR MAKING SHORT DOUGH

1. Combine the sugar and butter and mix only until it forms a smooth paste to ensure even blending. Do not mix vigorously so that air is incorporated.

2. Add the eggs gradually, a few at a time, and blend them in carefully. To prevent the mixture from breaking or curdling, have the eggs and any other liquid ingredients at room temperature, and blend them in carefully.

3. Add the dry ingredients and mix at low speed until just combined. Overmixing will make the dough tough.

4. *Turn out the dough onto a lightly floured work surface, shape it into a disk or flat triangle, and wrap tightly in plastic wrap. If the dough appears to be somewhat rough or coarse when it is removed from the mixer, work it gently by hand just until it comes together. Refrigerate before using to allow the dough to firm up and the gluten to relax. The butter becomes soft during the mixing process, making short dough difficult to work with immediately after mixing. Allowing the gluten to relax will create a more tender product.*

Pâte à Choux

Pâte à choux is a cooked batter created through the combination of liquid, butter, flour, and eggs. When finished it is piped into various shapes that, once baked, expand and dry into crisp hollow pastry.

THE BASIC STEPS FOR MAKING PÂTE À CHOUX

1. *Combine the liquid and fat and bring to a rolling boil. Usually either water or milk is used as the liquid in the batter, and the two yield very different results. Milk will cause the pastry to darken more quickly in the oven before it has dried out enough to become crisp; that, along with the solids present in the milk, will produce more tender, flavorful pastry. When water is used, the temperature of the oven can be manipulated, starting with a very high temperature to encourage full expansion, and then a lower temperature to dry out the pastries, creating a fully dried pastry that will be very crisp and light.*

2. *Add the flour all at once, stirring constantly to prevent lumps from forming, and continue to cook until the mixture pulls away from the sides of the pan.*

The type of flour is important. Flours with a higher percentage of protein are able to absorb more liquid and will allow for the addition of a greater amount of eggs, yielding a lighter finished product. Additionally, a flour with a higher protein content will develop more gluten strands, making a more elastic dough, which will also help create a lighter finished product. For these reasons, bread flour, which has a protein content of 12 to 13 percent, is best. All of the flour must be added to the boiling liquid at once and blended in very quickly to ensure the full hydration of the starch granules in the flour and the formation of a smooth paste. The mixture should be stirred quickly and vigorously. The precooking and agitation of the batter allows for greater moisture absorption as well as the development of the gluten in the flour, which creates light, crisp pastry.

3. *Transfer the mixture to the bowl of a mixer and, using the paddle attachment, mix for a few moments to cool the batter slightly.*

4. *Add the eggs gradually, in three or four additions, mixing the dough until it is smooth again each time. Scrape down the sides and the bottom of the bowl as necessary. The dough should have a pearl-like sheen and be firm enough to just hold its shape when piped.*

Strudel Dough

Strudel dough is a slightly enriched soft dough. Bread flour is used for strudel dough because of its higher protein content, which accounts for the development of the elasticity of the dough that allows it to be stretched to make thin layers of pastry. The dough is mixed well to develop the gluten and then allowed to rest in a warm place (cold dough has less elasticity and is therefore more difficult to work with). The dough is then stretched until extremely thin and transparent. Commercially made phyllo dough, another thin flaky dough, is often used in place of strudel dough.

Laminated Dough

Laminated doughs include croissant, puff pastry, and Danish dough. Proper layering (lamination) is vital, as it is the combination of fat and dough in even layers that causes expansion and creates the ultimate flaky texture characteristic of laminated doughs. When the dough is baked, the fat melts, creating pockets where released steam from the moisture in the dough acts to leaven the dough. As the steam leavens the pockets in between the dough layers, causing the product to expand and rise, the remaining fat "fries" the dough so that the air spaces are retained.

Creating the proper number of fat and dough layers is critical to the success of laminated doughs. With too few layers, the steam will escape and the pastry will not rise. Folding the dough too many times can be a problem because the layers of fat and dough merge together as the fat begins to become incorporated into the dough, rather than remaining as separate layers, thus preventing the dough from rising.

Folding may be the most important factor in making a laminated dough, as the distinct layers of fat and dough must be maintained throughout the process. The dough must be rolled out evenly and the corners kept squared throughout the lock-in (the stage at which the roll-in butter is introduced to the dough) and all subsequent folds to ensure proper layering.

THE BASIC STEPS FOR MAKING LAMINATED DOUGH

1. *Prepared dough (the initial dough) is folded and rolled together with a block of fat called a roll-in. To prepare the dough, sift together the flours. Blend in the butter on low speed with a dough hook attachment until pea-size nuggets form.*

2. *Combine the water and salt; add all at once to the dough, and mix on low speed until smooth. Dough that is to be laminated must be mixed carefully. Overmixing can result in too much gluten formation, making the dough elastic and difficult to roll out.*

3. *Shape the dough into a rough square or rectangle. The dough should be gently rolled into the desired shape for the lock-in before it is refrigerated to reduce the amount of manipulation necessary during lock-in and lamination. Transfer to a sheet pan lined with parchment paper, wrap the dough in plastic wrap, and allow it to relax under refrigeration for 30 to 60 minutes. While the dough is resting, prepare the roll-in fat.*

4. *To prepare the roll-in, the butter should be worked, either by hand or carefully using a stand mixer, until it is smooth and malleable but not overly soft. A number of different types of fats may be used in lamination. However, butter lends the best flavor and mouthfeel.*

5. *A small amount of flour may be added to the butter to make it easier to work with and to absorb excess moisture in the butter. Mix the butter and flour (if using) until smooth. It is important that the fat be completely smooth, as any lumps will tear the dough as it is rolled in, preventing proper layering.*

6. Transfer the roll-in to a sheet of parchment paper. Cover with a second sheet and roll into a rectangle. Square off the edges, cover with plastic wrap, and refrigerate until firm but still pliable. The temperature of the roll-in is very important. Do not allow it to become cold. It should be the same consistency as the dough when the two are rolled together. The butter must not be allowed to become so soft that it begins to ooze from the dough as it is rolled, nor should it be so firm that it could tear the dough or break into bits during rolling. Before use, the roll-in may be allowed to stand at room temperature for a few minutes if it is too hard, or re-refrigerated if it becomes too soft.

7. To lock the roll-in into the dough, turn out the dough onto a lightly floured work surface and roll it into a square or rectangle, if necessary, keeping the edges straight and the corners squared. The roll-in fat can be added to the dough using one of several methods: envelope, single-fold, or three-fold.

   For the envelope method, the dough is rolled into a square or a rectangle. The roll-in is rolled into a smaller square or rectangle, and placed diagonally in the center of the dough so that each corner points to the center of a side of the dough. The corners of the dough are then folded over the fat, envelope-style, so that they meet in the center.

   In the single-fold method, the roll-in is rolled into a rectangle that is half the size of the dough square or rectangle, and placed on one-half of the dough, then the other half of the dough is folded over it and the edges are sealed to completely encase the roll-in fat.

   In the three-fold method, the fat is rolled into a rectangle that covers two-thirds of the dough. The one-third of the dough not covered with the roll-in fat is folded over to cover half of the roll-in, or the center of the rectangle, and then the remaining side (or third) is folded over that. The edges are then sealed to completely encase the roll-in fat.

8. Administer a four-fold. Cover the dough in plastic wrap and allow it to rest for 30 minutes under refrigeration. For a four-fold or book-fold, divide the sheet of pastry visually into quarters, and fold the outer quarters into the middle so that their edges meet. Then fold the dough over as if closing a book. This type of fold quadruples the number of layers in the dough each time. Ideally, the edges from the initial fold to the center will be slightly off center.

9. Turn the dough 90 degrees from its position before it was refrigerated and roll it out into a rectangle, making sure the edges are straight and the corners are squared. Administer a second fold (three-fold or four-fold). Cover the dough in plastic wrap and allow it to rest for 30 minutes under refrigeration. Repeat this process two more times for a total of four folds, turning the dough 90 degrees each time before rolling and allowing the dough to rest, covered in plastic wrap under refrigeration, for 30 minutes between each fold.

   After the roll-in is added to the dough, each subsequent fold is usually either a three-fold or a four-fold. Each time, before folding and rolling the dough, brush any excess flour from its surface. When you fold the dough, the corners should squarely meet and the edges should be straight and perfectly aligned. After each fold, refrigerate the dough to allow it to relax and the butter to chill; the length of time the dough will need to rest will depend in large part on the temperature of the kitchen. For each fold, the dough is turned 90 degrees from the previous one to ensure that the gluten is stretched equally in all directions. Too much stress in one direction will make the dough difficult to roll and it may rise unevenly and become misshapen during baking as the gluten contracts.

10. After completing the final fold, wrap the dough in plastic wrap and allow it to rest under refrigeration for 30 minutes before using.

Three-Fold

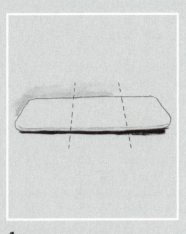

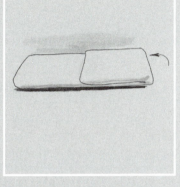

1 *Roll the dough to the proper dimensions and visualize it in thirds.*

2 *Fold one-third of the dough over the center third.*

3 *Fold the final third over the center. Refrigerate before rolling and folding again.*

Four-Fold

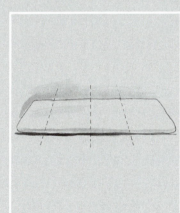

1 *Roll the dough to the proper dimensions and visualize it in uneven quarters.*

2 *Fold the two ends so they meet off center.*

3 *Fold the ends over to meet precisely. Refrigerate before rolling and folding again.*

PASTRIES

Pastry is a general term that encompasses a wide variety of products that may be traditional or contemporary, rustic or refined, simple or extremely complex. Pastries are very versatile and may be served as breakfast items, as components in sweet or savory applications, or as stand-alone desserts.

Tartlets

By scaling down the formulas for various pies and tarts, the pastry chef can prepare a number of in-dividual pastries. The same basic principles used for preparing large pies and tarts apply to tartlets. They can be baked in a mold or free-form (as with a galette). They may be made using short dough or puff pastry dough. Depending on the type of filling, the shells may be partially or completely prebaked. They may be filled with fresh or poached fruits, nuts, chocolate ganache, or custard. Many types of fillings contain components that combine techniques; for example, one component of a filling could be a fran-gipane filling, which would be baked with the crust, then jam could be added in a thin, even layer, and the tart finished by topping it with fresh berries or

When filling a tart or tartlet shell with dough, very carefully roll the dough off the rolling pin and into the pan, then trim off the excess dough.

other fruit. Combining elements in this way gives the pastry chef freedom to explore different flavor and textural profiles to create unique desserts. Prebaked tartlet shells should be left in the ring molds while they are filled, to support them during assembly and until the filling sets.

Layered Pastries and Roulades

Layered individual pastries can be composed of various types of cake or pastry that are baked as sheets so they can be layered or rolled with a complementary filling. Properly assembled, the evenly filled, level layers make a dramatic and visually appealing pastry when sliced. A variety of icings, such as ganache, buttercream, whipped cream, fondant, or a clear glaze, may be applied to the assembled pastry. These large layered pastries can be cut into a variety of shapes, such as triangles or rectangles, to make individual portions. Assembling pastries in this manner results in very little loss or trim, making them an economical choice for production. Many traditional, classic, and contemporary cakes can be adapted with only minor modifications to suit this style of assembly.

Roulades are made from a sheet of cake or other cake that is flexible enough to be rolled without splitting. The sheet of cake is spread with an even layer of filling and then rolled, chilled, iced, and decorated. The roulade is then sliced into individual portions for service. Roulades are easy to prepare and can be made ahead and finished as needed.

Pastries Formed in Molds

You can use a variety of small portion-size molds to shape such pastry components as mousse, Bavarian cream, and other stable creams. In most cases, gelatin is added to the cream to give it enough structure to hold its shape after it is unmolded. There are several styles and materials to choose from. One option is flexible molds made of silicone, produced in hemisphere, pyramid, and other shapes. Cups, bowls, and other small containers also work well. Combine components in a variety of colors, flavors, and textures; to add texture, consider small cookies, ladyfingers, sponge, or fresh fruit. To add color, include a garnish of a contrasting color.

Containers

Pastry chefs are often on the lookout for unusual and attractive containers for presenting and serving special pastries and other desserts. Glass containers have several appealing qualities. Clear glass gives a pastry an immediate visual impact. Stemmed coupe glasses, hurricane glasses, and oversized martini glasses automatically give the pastry height. Natural and edible containers, including hollowed-out citrus fruits and containers such as puff pastry cases (known as *vols-au-vent* or *bouchées*), pâte à choux puffs, and tuile cups, are all part of the classic pastry repertoire and can be other attractive choices.

Phyllo Dough Pastries

Phyllo dough is made only of flour and water (and occasionally a small amount of oil). The dough is stretched and rolled until it is extremely thin, then cut into sheets. The sheets are layered to create many flaky layers of pastry that encase or hold a filling, which may be anything from fruit to a mousse or cream. The finished layered dough is similar to a laminated dough, but instead of the fat being rolled into the dough as it is for laminated dough, the butter is melted and brushed onto the phyllo dough sheets before they are baked, as is done with strudel.

Many bakeshops purchase frozen phyllo dough sheets. This dough must thaw and come to room temperature before it can be worked with. Phyllo dough can dry out quickly and become brittle enough to shatter, so after it is removed from its wrapping, it is important to cover it with dampened towels and plastic wrap. Use a pastry brush to apply the butter in an even coat and then, if desired, sprinkle with cake or bread crumbs to keep the layers separate as they bake.

Silicone Molds

1 Silicone pyramid molds filled with chocolate cake with a pistachio insert.

2 After they are unmolded, the pyramid cakes are sprayed with melted chocolate using an airbrush.

Decorative Mats

1 An offset spatula is used to spread parfait onto a decorative mat to obtain a desired shape.

2 Once the parfait is set, the decorative mat is peeled away.

Piped Pastries

A variety of individual pastries can be made using meringue or pâte à choux. Both of these elements are shaped by piping, then baked and filled. Meringues can be piped into containers, filled, and served, or piped into disks and assembled like a sandwich. The fillings paired with meringue are usually high in fat to contrast with the lean flavor and crisp mouthfeel of the meringue. Pâte à choux can be piped into oblongs for éclairs, into rings for Paris-Brest, into domes for cream puffs, or into more intricate shapes to create classic swans and other shapes. After baking, a filling is piped into the choux pastries either by slicing it open or by using a small pastry tip to puncture the shell and inject the filling. Pastries of this type are typically glazed or dusted with confectioners' sugar to finish. It is important when preparing either type of shell (meringue or pâte à choux) that it be baked until dry and crisp and allowed to cool completely before filling.

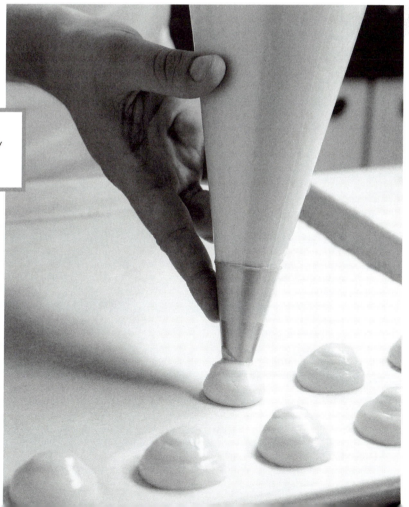

Once baked, piped pâte à choux becomes a crisp, hollow pastry. Here, it is piped into cream puffs.

Croissant and Danish Pastries

Croissants and Danishes have many similarities in ingredients and preparation method. They differ, however, in ratios of ingredients and application. Danish dough contains a higher percentage of fat and other enriching ingredients, which gives finished pastries made with this dough flakier layers. Danish dough is commonly used to prepare individual as well as larger cake-style pastries, while croissant dough is used only to produce individually sized items.

THE BASIC STEPS FOR SHAPING PREPARED CROISSANT AND DANISH DOUGHS

1. *To work with croissant and Danish doughs after they are prepared, keep the dough well chilled, taking out only the amount you can cut, fill, and shape in a relatively short amount of time because both doughs are yeast-raised. If the dough starts to warm as you work with it, you may lose some of the flaky, delicate texture that is the hallmark of a well-made Danish or croissant. The delicate and flaky texture desired of this product is created by maintaining distinct layers of fat and dough throughout the process; warm dough may result in overly softened butter that oozes out of the layers during rolling.*

2. *Use a sharp knife when shaping or cutting the dough. Clean cuts will ensure that the baked item rises evenly. To keep cuts even and straight when cutting by hand, use a straightedge as a guideline. Pastry wheels are helpful when cutting large quantities of dough. Croissant dough may be cut using specialty cutters. As the pastry is cut, you may create scraps or trim. These scraps can be reserved and rerolled for use in pastries where a high, straight rise is not critical. Scraps should be layered flat on top of each other, preserving the layers of fat and dough, and then rolled and stored under refrigeration or frozen.*

3. *After Danish or croissant doughs have been filled as desired and shaped, they are pan-proofed until nearly double in volume. Typically, they are lightly coated with egg wash. Depending upon the shaping and filling technique, Danish dough may be brushed with a clear fruit glaze or gel after baking for even greater moisture, flavor, and visual appeal. Using an egg wash creates a glossy, shiny crust.*

CAKES

Cakes are foundation preparations that are essential for any professional baker to master. Depending on the preparation, cakes can have a variety of textures from airy sponge cakes to dense fruit cakes. Cakes are often cut into layers and finished with a filling, icing, or fondant, but may also be cut into petits fours or assembled into a torte.

Traditional Wedding Cakes

Traditional British-style wedding cakes are perhaps the quintessential wedding cakes, from which most other wedding cake styles have derived. These are, in general, unfilled dark fruit cakes. The richness of the cake reflects a time when refrigeration was unavailable. Dried fruit, sugar, suet, and thick layers of coatings and icings helped the cakes stay fresh for one year, as the top layer would be saved and eaten on the couple's first anniversary. The cakes are traditionally coated with a layer of jam, then with marzipan, and finally with several coats of royal icing. The jam and marzipan keep the white icing from absorbing oils or moisture from the cake, while protecting the cake itself from moisture loss and staling.

Traditional British-style cakes consist of three tiers supported by pillars, generally pastillage, and both the icing and the decoration, which consists of royal icing piping and pastillage, are pure white. To some traditionalists, the British cake remains the only true wedding cake. Because the cake does not require refrigeration, which would damage sugar décor work, very detailed decorations (often baroque or gothic in style) can be applied. However, the labor-intensive nature of this style of cake is a drawback for most pastry chefs and bakers today—and these cakes are not to everyone's taste. In addition, the royal icing used for décor is very hard and brittle, making it difficult to cut such a cake cleanly or easily.

The British cultural influence is reflected in the styles of wedding cakes that evolved in countries colonized by Britain. The Australian and South African styles are shining examples of this influence. Decoration consists of minute royal icing piping and gum paste flowers. Colors, if used at all, are the softest of pastels. Although these cakes may be quite ornate, their overall appearance is very soft and delicate. The tiers may simply be stacked, supported on pillars, or, often, displayed on offset asymmetrical cake stands. In the Australian-style wedding cake, as with the British, it is not uncommon for tiers to be octagons, squares, or horseshoe shapes. The primary appeal of Australian cakes is their ornate yet delicate appearance. Beautiful realistic flowers are created from gum paste, and royal icing embroidery, string work, flood work, and ornaments are used to create stunning and intricate effects. The very detailed style of decoration, however, can be a disadvantage to the pastry chef or baker in that it is labor-intensive and therefore expensive to produce. The South African–style cake is very similar, but it can be distinguished from the Australian style by the large yet delicate wings made of royal icing filigree and flood work that extend over the cake.

The British cake also spawned American-style cakes. American wedding cakes are most clearly defined by the use of buttercream icing, buttercream piping décor, and buttercream roses, often colored. There is no single cake type of choice in American cakes, but pound cakes, high-ratio cakes, génoise, and carrot cakes are most common. Regardless of the style of cake, good judgment and craftsmanship are required for the production of a cake that is cost-effective and attractive. Highly decorated cakes such as these should always be made with high-quality ingredients so that the finished cake can be both a delicious dessert and an impressive showpiece.

Modern Wedding Cakes

Clean, straight lines and simple decorations in the form of cutouts of chocolate, pastillage, marzipan, or nougatine define contemporary wedding cakes. Fresh flowers or fresh fruits are frequently used. The cake itself may be almost any variety, from cheesecake to mousse cake to sponge with fruit, or even a charlotte. Almost any type of icing may be used, with whipped cream and good-quality buttercream being the most commonly used icings. Offset cake stands are the rule for modern cakes, since they are too light and fragile to be stacked.

The advantages of modern-style cakes are efficiency in production and visual and taste appeal. Simple elegance and a light, fresh appearance are the objectives, in contrast to the baroque ornamentation of more traditional styles. Cutouts can be made in advance, then placed on the cake relatively quickly for decoration. Fresh fruit and flowers are beautiful in their own right and require little assistance from the pâtissier. The taste of the finished product is an important factor in favor of the modern-style wedding cake, with virtually no restrictions on the type of cake or fillings. Generally, as with modern cuisine, fresh and seasonal products are employed to their best advantage. If a customer loves fresh strawberry charlotte, there is no reason the pâtissier cannot create a festive, attractive wedding cake composed of charlottes. Many people seek out the unusual, and a modern-style wedding cake can be tailored to their liking.

Specialty Cakes

Specialty cakes employ many of the same techniques as do wedding cakes. There are two elements that distinguish wedding cakes from specialty cakes: Specialty cakes are typically not tiered or stacked as are wedding cakes, and they are most often less ornately decorated. In some respects, however, the creation of a specialty cake presents fewer restrictions to the pastry chef's or baker's creativity. Specialty cakes are less limited by shape, color, and type of décor and can include cakes that are shaped like landmarks or cake layers that are stacked topsy-turvy. Types of décor for these cakes will be restricted only by ambient temperature and humidity.

Cake Finishing Techniques

BUTTERCREAM

Buttercream is an essential preparation in the pastry shop. Made with fresh sweet butter, natural flavorings, and other top-quality ingredients, it is excellent as a filling or icing for many cakes and pastries. There are four types of buttercream: Italian, Swiss, German, and French. Each has different characteristics that make them best suited for different applications.

A layer or coating of buttercream should be even and thin. It should completely cover the layer or outside of the pastry or cake without being excessively thick. It should add enough moisture, flavor, and texture to complement without overpowering the pastry or cake. Allow cold buttercream to come to room temperature before using. Then place it in the bowl of a mixer fitted with the paddle attachment and mix until smooth and spreadable.

Italian Buttercream

Italian buttercream is made with meringue, butter, and flavorings. The meringue may be either an Italian or Swiss meringue. The use of egg whites results in a relatively white-colored product that is very light in texture. The light color and texture of a finished Italian buttercream make it a common choice for wedding cakes or any pastries requiring white frosting.

Italian Buttercream

MAKES 6 LB 9 OZ/2.98 KG

INGREDIENT	U.S.	METRIC
Sugar	2 lb	907 g
Egg whites	1 lb	454 g
Water	8 fl oz	240 mL
Butter, soft	3 lb	1.36 kg
Vanilla extract	1 tbsp	15 mL
Flavoring	as needed	

1. Combine 8 oz/227 g of the sugar with the egg whites in the mixer bowl.

2. Combine the water with the remaining 1½ lb/680 g sugar in a saucepan. Cook the mixture until it reaches the soft ball stage (240°F/116°C).

3. When the sugar syrup reaches 230°F/110°C, begin whipping the egg whites on medium speed with the *whisk* attachment. The egg whites should reach soft peaks at the same time the sugar reaches the desired temperature.

4. Stream the hot sugar into the whipping whites. Continue whipping until cooled to room temperature.

5. While the meringue is cooling, cut the butter into 1-in/3-cm cubes.

6. Once the meringue is cool, switch to the paddle attachment and gradually add the butter on medium speed. Cream until smooth and light; flavor as desired.

THE BASIC STEPS FOR MAKING ITALIAN BUTTERCREAM

1. *Combine the sugar and water in a heavy-bottomed saucepan. A heavy-bottomed saucepan is used as it conducts heat most evenly. Bring to a boil over medium-high heat, stirring to dissolve the sugar. Continue cooking, without stirring, until it reaches the soft ball stage (240°F/116°C).*

2. *Whip the egg whites in a mixer fitted with the whisk attachment on medium speed until frothy. A whisk attachment is used as it best incorporates air into the product being mixed. Whip the meringue to medium peaks. It is important not to overwhip the meringue, for a stiff-peaked meringue is resistant to incorporation into other ingredients.*

3. *When the sugar syrup reaches 240°F/116°C, add it to the meringue in a slow, steady stream while whipping on medium speed. Whip on high speed until the meringue has cooled to room temperature.*

4. *Add the soft butter gradually, mixing until fully incorporated after each addition and scraping down the sides of the bowl as necessary. Scraping down the sides of the bowl ensures a thoroughly mixed, smooth buttercream. When using a mixer that doesn't touch the bottom of the bowl, make sure to additionally scrape the bottom as needed.*

5. *Blend in the vanilla. The buttercream is now ready for use or may be tightly covered and stored under refrigeration.*

Swiss Buttercream

The egg whites in a Swiss meringue buttercream are aerated through whipping, and stabilized by the dissolving sugar, creating a meringue that can be successfully incorporated with other ingredients. The combination of the fluffy consistency and the paleness of the Swiss meringue buttercream makes it ideal for use in wedding cakes and any pastries where a white buttercream is desired.

THE BASIC STEPS FOR MAKING SWISS BUTTERCREAM

1. *Place the sugar and egg whites in a stainless-steel bowl and whisk to combine. Set the bowl over a pan of barely simmering water and heat, whisking constantly, to 165°F/74°C. Whisking the sugar and egg whites over heat creates the Swiss meringue element of the buttercream.*

2. *Transfer the mixture to a mixer fitted with the whisk attachment and whip on high speed until the meringue is cool.*

3. *Gradually add the butter to the meringue while whipping on high speed; the buttercream should be light and creamy. Blend in the vanilla. The element of meringue in the buttercream creates a product that is light in texture as well as in color.*

4. *The buttercream is now ready for use or may be tightly covered and stored under refrigeration.*

German Buttercream

German buttercream is a combination of pastry cream, butter, and flavorings. The pastry cream contributes to the cream's yellow color. Because of its color, it is unsuitable for purposes where a white icing is desired. German buttercream has a richer texture than meringue-based buttercreams due to the whole eggs in the pastry cream.

THE BASIC STEPS FOR MAKING GERMAN BUTTERCREAM

1. *Cream together the butter and sugar until light and fluffy. The mixture of butter and sugar becomes fluffy due to the incorporation of air into the mixture through the creaming process.*

2. *Gradually add the pastry cream, mixing until fully incorporated after each addition and scraping down the sides of the bowl as necessary.*

3. *The buttercream is now ready for use or may be tightly covered and stored under refrigeration. German buttercream has a notably short shelf life and is unsuitable for being made in large batches and stored.*

French Buttercream

French buttercream is made with whole eggs and/or egg yolks, butter, cooked sugar syrup, and flavorings. It is similar to meringue-based Italian buttercream in technique, but the egg yolks make it richer and give it a yellow color.

THE BASIC STEPS FOR MAKING FRENCH BUTTERCREAM

1. *Whip the eggs in a mixer fitted with the whisk attachment on high speed until light and fluffy, about 5 minutes.*

2. *Combine the sugar and water in a heavy-bottomed saucepan. A heavy-bottomed saucepan is used as it conducts heat most evenly. Bring to a boil, stirring to dissolve the sugar. Continue cooking, without stirring, until the mixture reaches the soft ball stage (240°F/116°C).*

3. *Slowly pour the hot sugar syrup into the eggs while whipping on medium speed. Continue to whip until cool.*

4. *Gradually add the butter, beating until incorporated after each addition and scraping down the sides of the bowl as necessary. Scraping down the sides of the bowl ensures a thoroughly mixed, smooth buttercream. When using a mixer that doesn't touch the bottom of the bowl, make sure to scrape the bottom as needed.*

5. *Blend in the vanilla.*

6. *The buttercream is now ready for use or may be tightly covered and stored under refrigeration.*

Icing a Cake with Buttercream

1 Use a turntable for icing a cake. A turntable allows the cake to be rotated easily, which aids in the application of a smooth, even layer of buttercream. Use either a straight or offset metal spatula to ice the cake. The appropriate length of the spatula depends on the size of the cake and personal preference. After filling the cake, place a generous amount of buttercream on top. Hold a spatula steady and at a slight angle while spinning the turntable to apply a smooth even layer of buttercream on top of the cake. Allow the excess buttercream to fall down the sides of the cake.

2 To ice the sides of the cake, apply a generous amount of buttercream to the sides to ease smoothing and ensure a clean finish. To smooth the sides of the cake after applying the icing, hold a spatula vertically against the cake at a 45-degree angle, with the edge of the spatula touching the buttercream, and rotate the cake against the spatula; the tip of the spatula should just touch the surface of the turntable. This will not only smooth the buttercream, but will also cause some of the excess buttercream from the sides to rise above the top of the cake, making a lip or ridge.

3 Work from the edges of the cake toward the center. Hold the spatula against the top of the cake at a 45-degree angle and smooth the lip of buttercream over and across the top to create a perfectly smooth top and a sharp angled edge.

Flavoring Buttercream

Many different flavorings are compatible with buttercream. Of course, depending on the intended use, the amount of flavoring can be reduced or increased. Flavors may also be combined. It is often practical to make a large batch of buttercream and then flavor small portions as desired. Flavorings to be added to buttercream ideally should be at room temperature so they can easily be incorporated. Examples of flavorings include caramel, praline or other nut pastes, spices, fruit purées, citrus zest, and coffee extract.

Poured Fondant

Poured fondant is the traditional glaze for petits fours and doughnuts, among other pastries. Most kitchens and bakeshops use purchased fondant. For fondant to have its characteristic glossy finish, it must be warmed until it is liquid enough to flow readily (105°F/41°C). Small items are typically dipped into the fondant, using a dipping fork or similar tool. Larger items are set on racks placed on sheet pans and the fondant is poured, ladled, spooned, or drizzled over them. Assemble all your equipment before beginning, and keep the fondant warm as you work.

THE BASIC STEPS FOR USING POURED FONDANT

1. *Place the fondant in a stainless-steel bowl and place over a hot water bath to heat. Heating fondant reduces it to the liquid state needed to achieve the product's characteristically glossy finish. Do not let fondant exceed 105°F/41°C. Fondant should be warmed until it is able to flow readily.*

2. *Thin the fondant to the desired consistency with warm water, corn syrup, or another liquid such as liqueur.*

3. *If desired, color or flavor the fondant. Once it has been melted, plain fondant can be colored and flavored by adding coloring pastes, purées, concentrates, or chocolate. To make chocolate fondant, gradually add about 3 oz/85 g melted unsweetened chocolate to 1 lb/454 g warmed fondant. The amount of chocolate may be adjusted to suit the desired flavor and color.*

Rolled Fondant

Rolled fondant can be used to enrobe cakes, giving them a completely smooth, polished surface, and also to create cake décor like flowers, swags, and plaques.

It can be purchased premade or made in-house. If you're making your own rolled fondant, it is best to use it the same day it is made, as it will tighten up overnight. Rolled fondant can also be easily colored with liquid, paste, or powdered food coloring.

THE BASIC STEPS FOR COVERING A ROUND CAKE WITH ROLLED FONDANT

1. *Lightly dust the work surface with cornstarch. Roll the quantity of fondant you will need to completely cover the cake to ⅛ inch thick. To prevent the fondant from sticking to the surface as you roll, frequently turn the fondant and keep dusting with additional cornstarch.*

2. *Give the rolled fondant a good dusting with cornstarch, and, starting at one end, roll it up onto the rolling pin. Carefully unroll the piece of fondant over the cake, leaving equal amounts hanging on all sides of the cake.*

3. *Using your hands or a cake smoother tool, begin smoothing the top of the cake first, gently pushing out any air bubbles.*

4. *Once the top is completely smooth, begin pressing the fondant against the sides of the cake, starting at the top and working your way down the sides.*

5. *Once the fondant is completely adhered to all sides of the cake, use a cornstarch-dusted cake smoother to go over the entire cake with heavier pressure. This process should remove any remaining marks, lines, or wrinkles in the fondant. To remove any air bubbles that may remain under the layer of fondant, puncture them with a thin pin or needle and then smooth the area flat with the palm of your hand or a cake smoother.*

6. Using a paring knife, trim any excess fondant left around the bottom of the cake, so that the fondant is flush with the base.

7. To store, wrap the fondant-covered cake in plastic wrap and place in the refrigerator. Before removing the plastic wrap to finish and serve, allow the cake to return to room temperature.

TOOLS FOR PASTRIES, COOKIES, AND CAKES

There are a number of specialized tools that make preparing cakes, cookies, and pastries more efficient. Rolling pins, dough dockers, pastry cutters, and cookie cutters allow bakers to more quickly prepare dough for baking, while tools like offset spatulas, turntables, stencils, and cake combs aid with finishing.

CLOCKWISE FROM BOTTOM: Cake combs, offset spatulas, cake turntable, cooling rack (on bottom), sifter (on top).

CLOCKWISE FROM TOP: *Dough docker, pastry cutter, pastry brush, pastry wheel.*

Offset Spatulas

An offset spatula has a long metal blade, although the blade's edge is not sharp and it typically has blunt, rounded ends. The handle is angled so that the blade is about ½ inch below the handle. The spatulas can be used to spread fillings and icings or to gently lift and move cookies or pastry components.

Turntable

The cake turntable is also known as a lazy Susan. Essentially, it is a round flat disk, about 12 inches in diameter, which swivels freely on a pedestal base. Turntables are typically made out of cast iron or plastic. It is best to select a turntable with a relatively heavy base to prevent tipping while in use.

This tool is ideal for decorating cakes and constructing various pastries. It allows the baker to turn the cake on the disk with one hand while decorating with the other.

Cake Combs

Cake combs provide an easy way to decoratively finish the sides of an iced cake. They may be rectangular, triangular, or square and have serrated edges or teeth on each edge, and each edge will make a different pattern. Depending on the spacing and shape of the teeth, pulling a cake comb across the side of the iced cake can create smooth sides, lines, or wavy patterns. You can create a personalized version of a cake comb by using a sharp X-Acto knife to cut teeth into a plain plastic bench knife.

Cake combs can also be used to create white and dark chocolate striped cigarettes, and striped Joconde biscuits. They are ideal for creating designs for chocolate décor pieces as well.

Cake Spreader

Also known as an angel food cake cutter, a cake spreader is a metal tool that looks like a handled comb with long, thin teeth. It is used to cut very delicate cakes, such as angel food cake, because it is able to cut a piece from the whole without crushing the delicate crumb.

Dredger

A dredger is a small container with a fine-mesh lid that is filled with confectioners' sugar or cocoa powder to allow you to evenly dust cakes and other desserts.

Templates and Stencils

Templates and stencils can be used in many different applications, including making stenciled cookies, producing uniform bases for cakes and pastries, creating a pattern on Joconde sponge cake, and adding décor to the top of a cake, cookie, or pastry. Depending on its specific purpose, a template or stencil may be made of plastic, rubber, parchment, or cardstock.

A wide variety of shapes and sizes of premade stencils and templates is available at baking supply stores, but in most cases it's relatively easy and inexpensive to make your own. Simply draw or trace the desired design onto your chosen material and carefully cut it out using an X-Acto knife; this way you can create custom designs that perfectly fit your needs.

Docker

A dough docker is a handled roller studded with
1- to 2-inch rounded spikes of metal or plastic. The
docker is used to quickly and cleanly pierce holes in
rolled sheets of dough before blind baking to keep
the dough from rising. If you do not have a docker,
you can use a fork to accomplish the same purpose.

Bench Brush

A bench brush is a stiff-bristled brush that is used
to remove excess flour from work surfaces and from
the surface of dough.

Pastry Blender

A pastry blender consists of several semicircular
metal wires attached to a handle. It is used to blend
fat into flour when making a flaky pastry dough.

*Use a dough docker to prevent
dough from rising too high
during baking.*

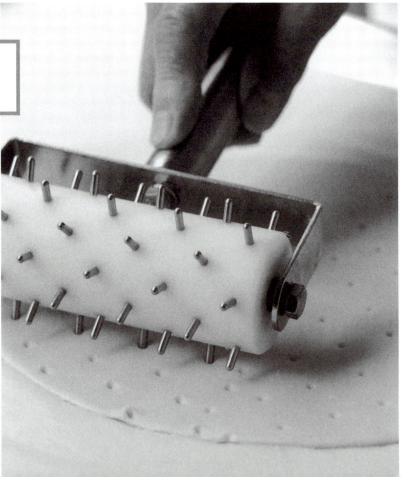

Pastry Wheel

A pastry wheel is a sharp, round nickel-plated blade attached to a handle. The wheel rotates as it is pushed over dough, making a long, smooth, and continuous cut. This tool is ideal for cutting raw pastry dough, sheets of puff pastry, gumpaste, and fondant. A pastry wheel can also be used to cut pieces for latticework, make score marks, or leave holes for venting. The wheel produces an even edge that can be straight or fluted.

Pastry Crimper Wheel

A pastry crimper wheel looks much like a pastry wheel with cutouts around the blade. When it is rolled over dough, it creates a scalloped edge. It is most often used on the edge of a raw pie crust to create the characteristic crimped edge.

Pastry Brushes

Pastry brushes may be made of soft, flexible nylon or unbleached natural bristles. The bristles are blunt cut and 2½ inches/6.25 centimeters long; the brushes come in a variety of widths for various tasks. They should be washed and air-dried after each use. Use when applying melted butter, oil, glazes, and egg washes.

Croissant Cutter

A croissant cutter is a cutting tool that, when rolled over sheeted croissant dough, produces triangular pieces of dough ready to be shaped into croissants. The blades are typically stainless steel, while its two handles may be metal, plastic, or wooden.

Petit Four Cutters

These small cutters are typically 1-inch across and 2-inches high, made of durable stainless steel. Press the cutter into the petit four base and gently remove. The most popular shape is a square, but cutters can be found in the shape of a rectangle, diamond, heart, half circle, eclipse, oval, circle, teardrop, and kidney. Petit four cutters can also be used to cut out small cookies or pieces of cheese.

Biscuit Cutters

Biscuit cutters are deep, round cutters used for cutting uniform circles out of biscuit dough, but they may also be used for cutting doughnuts, cookies, fritters, yeast dough buns, and other pastries. Biscuit cutters are made of stainless or tinned steel, and the cutting edges must be even and sharp enough to slice through the dough cleanly. Typically sold in sets of three, biscuit cutters may be plain-edged or fluted and may or may not have a handle.

Doughnut Cutters

Doughnut cutters are heavy-duty stainless- or tinned-steel tools used to cut doughnut dough. To create the traditional doughnut shape, each cutter consists of a larger circular blade (typically with a 2½- to 4-inch diameter) with a second, smaller circular blade (typically with a 1- to 1½-inch diameter) suspended in its center.

Cookie Cutters

Cookie cutters are used to stamp out individual cookies from rolled dough. They are made of plastic or thin sheet tin, stainless steel, or copper that has been molded or formed into shapes like circles,

CLOCKWISE FROM BOTTOM RIGHT: *Petit four cutters, biscuit cutters, fluted round cutters, doughnut cutter, cookie press with inserts, decorative cookie cutters.*

squares, hearts, animals, etc. The cutting edges must be even and sharp enough to slice through the dough cleanly, and the cutters should be easy to grip. Let the cutters dry thoroughly after use to prevent rusting, and dust with cornstarch before storing.

Cookie Press or Plunger

A cookie press, otherwise known as a cookie plunger, is a tool consisting of a hollow metal or plastic cylinder with disk-shaped stencils that fit tightly into one end; the cylinder is filled with cookie dough and a plunger, operated either manually or with a trigger, forces the dough through the stencil to create identical, pressed cookies.

Some traditional European cookies are made using special wooden molds that are also known as cookie presses. These intricate, hand-carved molds may be rolling cylinders or individual flat molds. When using this type of cookie press, the cookie dough is pressed into the wooden mold and turned out to create intricate, uniform cookies.

Ceramic Shortbread Molds

Ceramic shortbread molds are decorative, unglazed ceramic or stoneware forms traditionally used in the British Isles to make shortbread cookies. The molds vary in their exact design and shape but are usually about 7 to 10 inches in diameter. The shortbread dough may be pressed into the mold, immediately turned out, and baked on a sheet pan, or it can be baked in the ceramic mold and carefully turned out after it's cooled. (Always check to make sure that your mold is oven-safe before using in the oven.) The baked shortbread is then customarily cut into individual wedge- or diamond-shaped pieces for serving.

Rolling Pins

Rolling pins are used to thin and flatten doughs, such as yeasted bread, pastry, tart, and cookie doughs, as well as puff pastry, rolled fondant, and marzipan. They may be made of wood, metal, marble, or synthetic materials. Some pins have a smooth surface; others are textured or engraved to leave an impression of a pattern or picture on the dough. The task at hand will dictate the type of pin best suited for the job. Always clean and dry rolling pins thoroughly immediately after use. Pins made of porous materials such as wood may absorb the taste of soaps and detergents and transfer them to delicate doughs, so use only warm water and rub with a soft cloth to clean them. Never soak wooden pins in water for extended periods.

Rod-and-bearing rolling pins consist of a cylinder made of hardwood with a steel rod inserted through the middle, which is fixed with ball bearings and handles at either end. These heavy pins are used to roll large amounts of stiff dough. They are available in lengths up to 18 inches/45 cm. Pins of this style are also available with a cylinder made of stainless steel or marble. These materials remain cool during rolling, which helps to keep pastry dough at the proper working temperature.

Straight, or French, rolling pins are straight thick dowels. They were traditionally made of hardwood and now are also available in nylon and aluminum. These pins are typically 1¼ to 2 inches in diameter and 18 to 20 inches long. Because they don't have handles, they allow the baker or pastry chef to more easily feel the evenness and thickness of the dough while rolling it out.

Tapered rolling pins are thicker in the center and taper evenly to both ends. They are usually about 2½ inches in diameter at the center and 22 inches long. Their tapered design makes them most useful for rolling circles of dough to line pie and tart pans.

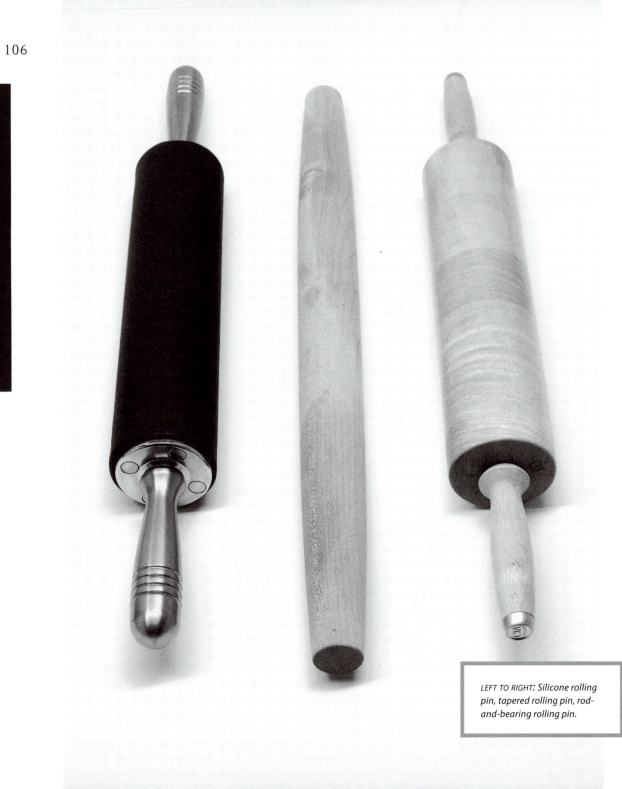

LEFT TO RIGHT: *Silicone rolling pin, tapered rolling pin, rod-and-bearing rolling pin.*

1-2-3 Cookie Dough

MAKES 6 LB/2.72 KG

INGREDIENT	U.S.	METRIC
Sugar	1 lb	454 g
Butter, soft	2 lb	907 g
Vanilla extract	1 tbsp	15 mL
Eggs, at room temperature	8 oz	227 g
Cake flour, sifted	3 lb	1.36 kg

1. Cream together the sugar and butter with the paddle attachment, starting on low speed and increasing to medium speed, scraping down the bowl periodically, until smooth and light in color, about 5 minutes.

2. Combine the vanilla and eggs and add them gradually, scraping down the bowl and blending until smooth after each addition. Turn off the mixer and add the flour all at once. Mix on low speed until just blended. Do not overmix.

3. Turn out the dough onto a lightly floured work surface. Scale the dough as desired. Wrap tightly and refrigerate for at least 1 hour before rolling. Cut or shape as desired.

A rod-and-bearing rolling pin is used to roll out cookie dough before cutting it with a cookie cutter.

Pie Weights

When blind baking a pie crust, the unfilled shell is lined with parchment paper and weighted down with pie weights to prevent the bottom of the crust from bubbling up and the sides from collapsing or sliding down the sides of the pan during baking. Pie weights may be ceramic or metal and are usually ball-shaped (either loose or connected in a chain). If pie weights are not available, you can use dried beans to accomplish the same purpose.

Ruler

A flat, metal ruler 12 to 16 inches in length is a handy tool to have in any bakeshop. It is useful for checking thicknesses, marking dough, and making straight cuts.

Wooden and Metal Skewers

Skewers, or thin, rounded sticks of wood or metal with pointed ends, are useful not only for grilling and for sweets served "on a stick," but also for testing the doneness of cakes and baked custards. A skewer carefully inserted into the center of a baked cake should come out clean, with no uncooked batter sticking to it; a skewer carefully inserted into the center of a baked custard should be moist but not wet or gooey.

7

CHOCOLATE, DÉCOR, AND CONFECTIONERY

Once mastered, good confectionery skills open the door to a nearly limitless repertoire of small bites and sweet treats. Chocolates and confections are particularly sensitive in terms of time, temperature, and ingredients and even the slightest change in method can affect the outcome of a product. The precision required for great confections is achieved through the application of practiced skill and good equipment. Accurate thermometers will result in chewy caramels, dipped cleanly in perfectly tempered chocolate with a sturdy dipping fork. Finished, these gems are the mark of a talented craftsman.

CHOCOLATE

Chocolate is perhaps the most complex ingredient in a baker's pantry. In matching a chocolate to a specific use, specific flavor nuances must be taken into account, not just whether it is dark or milk chocolate. For example, chocolate with fruity flavor notes might be more appropriate with a fruit-flavored ganache, while a dark-roasted, earthy chocolate might better complement a hazelnut cake. The following sections will detail how to work with chocolate.

Melting Chocolate

Melted chocolate can be used for a variety of purposes, but one of the most common is tempering chocolate. In order to properly temper chocolate, it must first be melted properly. If overheated, the quality of the chocolate is completely ruined.

THE BASIC STEPS FOR MELTING CHOCOLATE

1. *Chocolate that is to be melted should be finely chopped. The smaller the pieces, the more surface area is exposed, and the quicker the chocolate melts, helping to prevent overheating. This is an important consideration, as overheating chocolate will render it unusable. A heavy chef's knife is generally best for chopping chocolate, but some pastry chefs prefer to use a long serrated knife because the serrated blade breaks the chocolate into fine shards ideal for melting.*

2. *A hot water bath is usually used for melting chocolate, but it is important that moisture (steam, water, condensation) never comes in contact with the chocolate. Moisture causes the chocolate to "seize," or to become thick and grainy, rendering it unfit for tempering and most other uses. For this reason, it*

is important that the bowl (or the top of a double boiler) be completely dry and that the bowl (or top) fits snugly over the pan of water, forming a tight seal.

3. *The water should be steaming hot but not simmering.*

4. *Gently stir the chocolate occasionally as it melts. This ensures even heating and melting.*

5. *Remove the chocolate from the heat promptly once it is fully melted. This will keep the chocolate from becoming overheated.*

A microwave may also be used to melt chocolate. Some pastry chefs consider it the best choice because the chocolate does not come near water. The chocolate must be chopped or broken into small pieces about the same size. Use medium power rather than high, and heat the chocolate for 30-second intervals, removing and stirring after each to ensure even heating and melting.

Tempering Chocolate

Chocolate is purchased in temper, but in order to work with it, it must be melted and then tempered again, so that as it cools and sets it will return to the same state as when purchased. Tempered chocolate has the snap and gloss associated with good chocolate and will store better and for a longer period of time. Dipping or coating confections in tempered chocolate adds flavor, improves appearance, and helps to preserve them, as the tempered chocolate prevents moisture migration and keeps the filling from coming in contact with the air, which can cause spoilage.

Tempering is accomplished through a specific process of cooling and agitation. There are several different methods of tempering chocolate, such as the seed method, block method, and tabling method

WORKING WITH COUVERTURE

Couverture is chocolate that contains a minimum of 32 percent cocoa butter. This means it is thinner when melted than other chocolates and can easily form a thin coating, making it ideal for dipping and enrobing confections.

The temperature of the workspace and the temperature of the items to be coated are important factors in ensuring that tempered couverture retains its smooth, glossy appearance when set. When coating or dipping items in couverture, recrystallization must take place within a specific period of time. The ambient temperature should be between 65° and 70°F/18° and 21°C. The item to be dipped or enrobed should also be at room temperature. Confections that are too warm could cause the chocolate to bloom or to have a matte finish, while items that are too cold could "shock" the couverture, resulting in a dull finish.

described below, but all are based on the same general principles. Chocolate contains different types of fat crystals. When tempering chocolate, the object is to get the right type of crystals to form. Otherwise, when the chocolate sets, it will lack hardiness, snap, and shine, and will bloom. First, the chocolate must be heated to the correct temperature to ensure that all the different types of fat crystals melt: 110° to 120°F/43° to 49°C for dark chocolate, and 105° to 110°F/41° to 43°C for milk chocolate and white chocolate. A portion of chocolate that is already in temper is then added to "seed" the untempered chocolate and begin the formation of the beta crystals (the desirable stable fat crystals). Then the chocolate must be cooled to about 80°F/27°C while being constantly agitated. It is gradually brought back up to the appropriate working temperature. Whenever tempering chocolate, it is best to melt more than you will need, as it is easier to keep larger amounts of chocolate in temper.

For any method of tempering you choose, it is wise to test the chocolate when finished, making sure that it is in full temper. To do this, dip a tool such as a small spatula into the chocolate and set it aside. Continuing to gently stir the tempered chocolate, examine how the chocolate cools on the spatula. Properly tempered chocolate should set within 3 to 5 minutes at room temperature, and should be streak-free with a satiny shine. Chocolate not in full temper may be streaky, speckled, and dull, and will set more slowly; if this occurs the chocolate needs to be seeded further until full temper is achieved.

Tempered chocolate sets quickly. Working with relatively large amounts helps to keep it from cooling and setting too rapidly. If tempered chocolate begins to set and thicken as you work, act quickly so the chocolate will not have to be melted and re-tempered: Stirring constantly, hold the bowl of chocolate directly over a burner for 2 to 3 seconds; remove the chocolate from the heat while continuing to stir.

Repeat the process, checking the temperature of the chocolate each time after removing the bowl from the heat so the chocolate does not overheat and come out of temper, until the chocolate is again at the optimal working temperature and consistency. Be careful not to return the bowl to the heat until the bottom of the bowl feels cooler than body temperature.

Following are the three most common methods used to temper chocolate.

THE BASIC STEPS OF THE SEED METHOD

1. *Chopped tempered chocolate—approximately 25 percent of the weight of the melted chocolate to be tempered—is added to the warm (110°F/43°C) melted chocolate and gently stirred to melt and incorporate it. The stable crystals in the chopped chocolate help stimulate the formation of stable beta crystals in the untempered chocolate.*

2. *The whole mass is then brought to the appropriate working temperature.*

Stirring tempered chocolate into melted chocolate will bring it to temper using the seed method.

THE BASIC STEPS OF THE BLOCK METHOD

1. With the block method of chocolate tempering, a single block of tempered chocolate is added to warm melted chocolate and gently stirred until the desired temperature is reached. The block of chocolate not only reduces the temperature of the melted chocolate, but also provides the seed crystals necessary for tempering.

2. After the chocolate is brought into temper, the seed, or block of chocolate, is removed. The block can be used again. This method is simple and effective, but slightly more time-consuming than other methods of tempering.

THE BASIC STEPS OF THE TABLING METHOD

1. Approximately one-third of the melted chocolate (at 110°F/43°C) is poured onto a marble surface and spread back and forth with a spatula and scraper until it begins to thicken. A marble surface is used because it has a high thermal mass and, therefore, is most efficient in pulling heat from the chocolate.

2. As the tabled chocolate begins to set, the beta crystals form and it becomes dull and takes on a paste-like consistency. This resulting mass is then added to the remaining melted chocolate and gently stirred to seed the chocolate with the stable beta crystals.

3. The whole mass is then gradually brought to the appropriate working temperature.

Molding Chocolates

Couverture is always used for molding, as its high percentage of cocoa butter makes for a more fluid chocolate. The tempered chocolate used to fill the molds should be as warm as possible within the ideal working temperature range.

THE BASIC STEPS FOR MOLDING CHOCOLATES

1. Clean and allow the molds to come to room temperature. Chocolate molds should be completely clean and at room temperature before use. They should always be polished with a clean soft cloth to remove any debris or water spots, which would give the surface of the unmolded chocolate a blotchy or dull appearance. The temperature of the mold is also important. If a mold is cold, the chocolate will set too quickly; if the mold is warm, it may bring the chocolate out of temper.

2. When using molds that have an intricate design, first brush some of the chocolate into the mold. Brushing forces chocolate into the crevices of the design, ensuring that the detail of the mold will show clearly when the chocolate is unmolded.

3. Pour the tempered chocolate into the mold, completely filling it.

4. Working quickly, tap or vibrate the mold to release any air pockets and to ensure that the chocolate fills all the crevices.

5. Immediately invert the mold, pouring the excess chocolate back into the container of tempered chocolate, leaving only a thin coating in the mold. Do not reinvert the mold, or chocolate may pool, creating a layer of chocolate that is too thick. Instead, suspend the mold upside down by balancing the edges on two containers or bars over a sheet of clean parchment paper and let stand until the chocolate in the mold reaches a semisolid consistency.

6. To clean the surface of the mold, hold the mold at a 45-degree angle, bracing one edge against a flat surface; starting halfway up the mold, push a bench scraper down the mold, removing any chocolate on or above the surface of the mold. The edges of the chocolate must be flush with the surface of the mold so that the chocolate can be properly sealed after filling. If the chocolates are not properly sealed, they will have a shorter shelf life. Turn the mold around and remove excess chocolate from the other half.

7. Fill the mold 80 to 90 percent full with the desired filling, which must be liquid enough so that there is no possibility of creating air pockets.

8. Once it is filled, tap or vibrate the mold to release any air bubbles and settle the filling.

   To ensure that the mold is not overfilled, hold the mold up at eye level and look across the surface; there should be no filling visible above the surface. Any excess filling should be removed before the seal

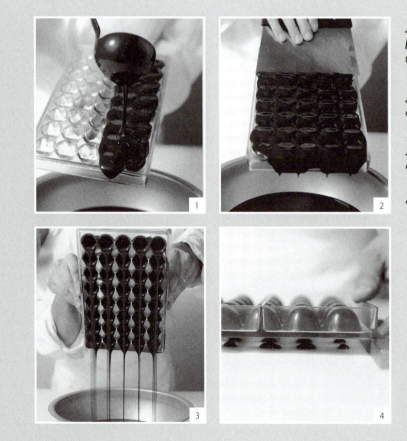

1 Ladle or deposit chocolate into clean, dry, polished molds, making sure to fill them to capacity.

2 Remove the excess chocolate from the top of the molds using a scraper or palette knife.

3 Invert the mold over a bowl to drain off the excess chocolate. This creates a thin outer shell.

4 Elevate the inverted mold slightly and allow the shells to set in their cast.

coat of chocolate is applied, or the filling will become mixed into the chocolate, which will not harden or effectively seal the confection.

9. Coat and seal the molded confections by drizzling on a thin layer of tempered chocolate, then gently spreading the chocolate out to cover and completely seal.

10. Let stand until the chocolate is in a semisolid state (it should be wet and tacky but not fluid), then clean the surface of the mold using a bench scraper as described above.

11. Chill molded chocolates under refrigeration for 5 to 10 minutes; do not freeze. To test whether the chocolates are ready to be unmolded, give the tray a slight twist; you should hear a crackle. With clear plastic molds, you can check the underside to see if the chocolates are releasing.

12. To unmold, turn the mold upside down and, holding it at a 45-degree angle, gently but firmly tap it once. Molded chocolates must be handled carefully at every step of the process. Even when finished, the chocolates can be damaged easily; picking up fingerprints, smudges, scratches, and the like will render a delicious product visually unappealing.

Ganache

CREAM GANACHE

Cream ganache has a wide range of uses, from filling centers for confections to glazing and filling cakes and pastries. In confectionery work, cream ganache is most commonly used as the center for truffles, but other confections are made with ganache as well. The consistency of ganache may be hard, soft, or any variation in between, depending on the ratio of chocolate to cream. Soft ganache and medium ganache are not firm enough, nor do they have an adequate shelf life, to be used in confectionery work. As a rule, hard ganache is required for piped and rolled truffle centers. Chocolate and cream are the basic ingredients for making ganache, but other ingredients may be added for flavoring and to provide a smoother texture. The addition of butter and/or corn syrup or glucose syrup can yield a superior finished product in both flavor and texture. Butter is added to the ganache to increase fat content when some of the cream in the formula is replaced with liqueur. Typically, the amount of butter to be added is half the weight of the liqueur. The butter is usually added to the ganache after the chocolate is fully melted. Light corn syrup or glucose syrup may be added to ganache to help prevent recrystallization of the sugar and maintain a smooth texture. The weight of the added corn syrup generally should not exceed 10 percent of the total weight of the ganache. Light corn syrup is typically added to the cream before it is boiled.

THE BASIC STEPS FOR MAKING A CREAM GANACHE

1. Chop the chocolate into small pieces of uniform size so the pieces will melt quickly and at the same rate. Dark, milk, or white chocolate may be used to make cream ganache. Milk and white chocolate contain

less cocoa solids and less cocoa butter than a dark variety and so require a higher recipe ratio of chocolate to cream. Percentages of cocoa solids or butter may also vary based on the chocolate manufacturer, so ratios should be adjusted as needed.

2. *Bring the heavy cream to a boil in a heavy-bottomed saucepan.*

3. *Pour the hot cream over the chocolate. Let the mixture stand undisturbed for a few minutes to allow the hot cream to begin melting the chocolate. When combining the chocolate and cream, some pastry chefs add the chocolate directly to the pan of hot cream; however, this practice risks scorching the chocolate on the bottom of the hot pan.*

4. *Stir the mixture gently to blend and melt the chocolate completely without incorporating air. If the chocolate is not fully melted at this point, warm the ganache over simmering water, stirring gently. When making ganache to be tabled, it is advisable to allow the boiled cream to cool to 170°F/77°C in order not to melt all the stable cocoa butter crystals.*

BUTTER GANACHE

Butter ganache is most commonly used as centers for confections. The sweetener used for butter ganache must be smooth—that is, its texture must not be discernable on the palate, because the mixture does not contain enough moisture to melt the sweetener. Examples of sweeteners well suited for making butter ganache are jam, corn syrup, glucose syrup, and fondant. The amount of sweetener used may equal as much as half the weight of the butter. The basic ratios for butter ganache are 2:1 or 2½:1 chocolate to butter. Spirits and liqueurs added for flavoring should be added last. When adding spir-

its, be careful to maintain the 2:1 or 2½:1 ratio of chocolate to butter; the spirit is calculated as part of the butter. To maintain the ratio, you can reduce the amount of butter or recalculate the quantity of chocolate based on the new value of butter plus spirit.

Butter ganache may be either piped or spread into a slab and cut to form confections. The butter is treated differently depending on which of the two techniques is used. If the ganache is to be piped, the butter is creamed with the sweetener until light and aerated. If the ganache is to be spread out into a slab to harden and be cut, the butter is blended with the sweetener, incorporating as little air as possible; if too much air is incorporated into the butter, the ganache is likely to crack when cut. Butter ganache must be worked with quickly and in small batches. Once it has set, it is very difficult to bring butter ganache back to a working consistency, as softening would require heat and that would ruin the structure by melting the butter.

THE BASIC STEPS FOR MAKING A BUTTER GANACHE

1. *Mix a sweetener with the softened butter.*

2. *Add the tempered chocolate and flavoring. The chocolate must be in temper when it is added to the butter or the butter ganache will not set properly.*

FLAVORING GANACHE FOR TRUFFLES

THE BASIC STEPS FOR INFUSING FLAVOR INTO CREAM GANACHE

1. *Bring the cream to a boil, add the flavoring, and remove the pan from the heat. Examples of common flavorings to be infused into ganache include vanilla, coffee, teas, and spices.*

2. Cover and allow to stand until the flavor has been infused into the cream, 5 to 10 minutes.

3. After steeping, aromatics such as teas, herbs, and spices are strained out of the cream.

4. After straining, water or milk should be added as necessary to bring the liquid to its original weight so the finished ganache will be the proper consistency.

5. Before the infused cream is added to the chocolate, it should be rewarmed so it is hot enough to melt the chocolate. A liqueur or other spirit may be added for flavoring. Pastes and compounds may also be used. Because these are strongly flavored, they are usually added to taste to the finished ganache.

Coating Truffles in Tempered Chocolate

One of the distinguishing characteristics of a high-quality truffle is a thin outer coating of tempered couverture. Two coats of chocolate should always be applied, a precoat and a final coat. As the outer shell of tempered chocolate coating hardens, it contracts and tightens around the ganache center, sometimes developing small cracks that allow the ganache or sugar within to seep out of the shell. Precoating truffles can prevent this from happening; it also makes the centers easier to handle and prolongs the shelf life of the final product.

THE BASIC STEPS FOR COATING TRUFFLES IN TEMPERED CHOCOLATE

1. To precoat a truffle, smear a small amount of tempered chocolate over the palm of your hand and gently roll the ganache center in the chocolate. It is important, with each coat, to use only enough chocolate for a thin coating; this reduces the chance of the truffles developing feet (chocolate that pools

around the base). Set the coated truffle on a parchment paper–lined sheet pan and repeat the process with the remaining truffles. Allow the precoat to set completely before applying the second, final coating.

2. Apply the final coat of chocolate in the same manner as the precoat, but make a thicker coat by using more chocolate.

Using Premade Chocolate Shells

Premade shells are consistent in shape and size, time efficient, and easier to package due to their uniformity. Of course, the cost and quality of the shells must be taken into consideration. Typically, premade shells are used for fillings too soft to be formed by piping or rolling. The shells must be filled carefully and completely because any small air pockets will allow mold to grow. Additionally, although hollow shells permit the use of soft fillings, you must be mindful of the water content of fillings and their potential for spoilage. After the shells are filled, they are capped with chocolate. The cap should extend over the edges of the hole in the shell so that as it hardens and contracts it will remain attached to the shell.

Dipping Confections in Tempered Chocolate

THE BASIC STEPS FOR DIPPING CONFECTIONS IN TEMPERED CHOCOLATE

1. To dip a center, place it in the tempered chocolate, slip the dipping fork under the confection in the chocolate, and, with a scooping motion, pick it up so that it is sitting right side up on the fork. When dipping confections, make sure to use a bowl of chocolate large enough to immerse them easily.

2. Gently raise and lower the confection on the fork a few times, allowing the base to just touch the surface of the melted chocolate. This removes excess chocolate from the dipped confection, so a foot does not form. (A foot occurs when excess chocolate pools around the base of the confection.)

3. Remove the confection from the bowl, gently scraping it on the edge of the bowl to remove any remaining excess chocolate from the base and to slide the confection so that one edge is hanging over the end of the fork. This is done to facilitate a clean and easy transfer of the product from the fork to the sheet pan.

4. Carefully lower that edge of the confection onto the clean parchment paper–lined sheet pan and gently pull the fork out from under the confection.

The front of each dipped confection is placed on the tray and the fork is slid out from underneath it.

Techniques for Finishing Chocolates

Décor is important in confectionery not only for eye and taste appeal, but also as a means of differentiating one filling from another. A dusting of cocoa powder is the classic finishing technique for truffles, but they can also be dusted with confectioners' sugar. Truffles and other round confections can also be rolled in a garnish, such as chocolate shavings or curls, chopped nuts, or toasted flaked coconut. *Spiking,* or rolling a just-dipped truffle on a wire screen, is another option that creates an erratic but aesthetically pleasing spiked surface. When spiking truffles, be sure to remove them from the screen before the chocolate sets completely.

Decorated transfer sheets can be applied to the top of any smooth, flat confection. After the confection has been dipped, immediately lay the transfer sheet on its surface. After the coating is completely set, remove the sheet.

Another common décor for flat confections is made with a dipping fork. After the confection has been dipped, allow it to set for a moment, and then touch the fork to its surface, lifting the chocolate up to create small waves.

Rochers

A rocher is a confection made from an item bound in tempered chocolate; typically, rochers are made from toasted nuts, but they can also be made with dried fruits or even cereal flakes. The ideal rocher is shaped like a haystack. The individual shapes of the nuts or candied fruit should be clearly visible through the chocolate. Tossing the nuts or fruit with melted cocoa butter before adding the chocolate will act to thin the chocolate and give more definition to the shape of the nuts or fruits. Work quickly and in small batches when making rochers. If the chocolate is too firm when it is deposited, the confections will not hold together and will have a dull finish.

Dragées

Dragées are nuts coated with cooked sugar and are typically coated in chocolate. To ensure the desirable thin coating of caramel, only a relatively small amount of sugar is used when making dragées. The larger the nut, the less sugar you should use, and the nuts used for dragées should not be toasted, as they will roast as the sugar caramelizes. Typical proportions by weight vary from 3 parts nuts to 1 part sugar for small nuts to 6 parts nuts to 1 part sugar for large nuts.

CONFECTIONS

Sugar can be manipulated in different ways to create a wide variety of confections, including hard candy, toffee, brittle, jellies, fudge, cordials, nougat, rock candy, and pralines.

Cooking Sugar

When cooking sugar, all your equipment must be clean and free of any grease. The sugar must also be free of impurities, such as flour or other ingredients. Sugar has a very high caramelization point and any impurities in the sugar are likely to burn at a much lower temperature, before the sugar begins to caramelize. A copper or other heavy-bottomed saucepan should be used to ensure constant, even heat. Sugar may be cooked by one of two methods: wet or dry. When cooking or caramelizing sugar by either method, a small amount of an acid (typically lemon juice at approximately ¼ tsp/1.25 mL for 8 oz/227 g of sugar) can be added to help prevent crystallization during cooking.

Regardless of the cooking method, when caramelizing sugar, it is important to stop the cooking process by shocking the pan in an ice water bath just as, or just before, it reaches the desired color. Sugar retains heat and can easily become too dark or burn if the cooking process is not arrested. It is also important to heat any liquids to be added to the caramel and to add them carefully. Caramelized sugar is very hot and will splatter when a colder ingredient is introduced.

WET METHOD

Of the two techniques for cooking sugar—wet and dry—only the wet method allows the sugar to be cooked to and used at the various stages that are vital for countless preparations. The dry method of sugar cooking melts the sugar crystals by the application of heat, resulting in sugar that caramelizes almost as soon as it melts. The wet method of sugar cooking, however, dissolves the sugar in water; then as the solution cooks, the water evaporates, acting to increase the concentration of sugar and resulting in a supersaturated, noncrystalline sugar solution. The concentration of the sugar solution increases as the solution is cooked, the temperature increases, and more of the water evaporates.

Sugar Stages and Temperatures

STAGE	DEGREES FAHRENHEIT (°F)	DEGREES CELSIUS (°C)
Thread	215°–230°	102°–110°
Soft Ball	240°	116°
Firm Ball	245°	118°
Hard Ball	250°–260°	121°–127°
Soft Crack	265°–270°	129°–132°
Hard Crack	295°–310°	146°–154°
Caramel	320°	160°

When cooking sugar, use clean water and a pastry brush to wash down any crystals that form on the inside of the pot.

THE BASIC STEPS OF THE WET METHOD OF COOKING SUGAR

1. *Combine the sugar in a saucepan with 30 percent or more of its weight in water. The sugar is intended to dissolve in the added water; if not enough water is added the result may be undissolved sugar crystals in the syrup that in turn could cause recrystallization.*

2. *Place the pan over high heat and stir constantly until the mixture comes to a boil to ensure that all the sugar is melted. As the dissolved sugar is heated, the water evaporates, acting to increase the concentration of sugar; as the temperature increases, water continues to evaporate, leaving behind a supersaturated non-crystalline sugar solution.*

   Stirring constantly is important as agitation will prevent the collision of particles in the solution that leads to crystallization.

3. *Once it has come to a boil, stop stirring and skim off any impurities.*

4. *Using a pastry brush, wash down the sides of the pan with cool water to prevent crystals from forming. Crystallization of the cooking sugar occurs readily on the side of the pan where crystals are deposited from evaporating liquid. These crystals, in turn, can easily act to "seed" the rest of the sugar in the pan, causing it to begin to crystallize, becoming lumpy and granular. Repeat as often as necessary to keep the sides of the pan clean until the sugar has reached the desired temperature, consistency, and color. A "seed" in this context is anything that will act as a surface hosting the growth of sugar crystals. Examples of seeds are whole sugar crystals, air bubbles, or skewers (as sometimes used in making candy). Brushing the inner sides of the pan with cool water prevents crystals from forming by adding moisture lost in evaporation during cooking.*

Dry Method

The dry method is used exclusively for caramelizing. The characteristically nutty and roasted flavor of caramel is best achieved through the use of this method.

THE BASIC STEPS OF THE DRY METHOD OF COOKING SUGAR

1. *Add a small amount of the sugar to a preheated medium-hot pan set over medium heat and allow it to melt.*

2. *Add the remaining sugar in small increments, allowing each addition of sugar to fully melt before adding the next. Continue this process until all of the sugar has been added to the pan. Cook to the desired color. Using this method, sugar crystals are melted through the application of heat, resulting in sugar that caramelizes almost as soon as it melts. Because it cooks so quickly, it is important to monitor the sugar constantly.*

Making Soft Caramels

If the mixture for caramels is undercooked, the caramels will be too soft and will not have the proper caramel flavor. If it is overcooked, they will be too firm. Although a thermometer is helpful in making caramels, the final assessment of whether the caramel is ready should be determined by testing the batch using ice water and a spoon. If the caramel is too firm, more liquid can be added to adjust the consistency. Soft caramels may be flavored in any number of ways. Strong flavorings such as coffee beans, hazelnut paste, or spices can be added to the cream at the beginning of the cooking process. To make fruit caramels, replace up to half of the liquid in the recipe with a fruit purée. When using a fruit purée, it is advisable to cut the amount of glucose syrup by half, and it is likely that you will have to cook the caramels to a higher temperature to achieve the same consistency, due to the acidity of the fruit and the reduced amount of milk solids in the formula.

Making Peanut Brittle

Some caution is necessary when making peanut brittle. Temperature and color must be carefully monitored to achieve the characteristic flavor and texture. If your peanut brittle is pale or milky white and granular, it probably was either not cooked to a high enough temperature or was stirred too much and/or too rapidly during cooking. Peanut brittle demands a slow, steady stir, especially after the peanuts have been added. As a general rule, if the mixture has reached the proper temperature but the color is not fully developed, continue cooking to the desired color.

Making Hard Candies

Oils, extracts, and concentrated synthetic or natural flavors are the most common flavorings used for hard candies. These flavorings are added at the end of the cooking process because they are often not heat-stable and because any acid they contain will prevent the finished product from becoming completely hard. Hard candies can be poured onto a slab, partially cooled, and then pulled and cut, or they can be cast in starch molds or other types of molds.

DÉCOR

Décor is the finishing touch given to any pastry or cake. Gum paste, pastillage, modeling chocolate, and marzipan are all edible substances that can be rolled, molded, and modeled like clay; flowers, fruit, ropes, figures, plaques, and other shapes created from these media are often used to decorate cakes, cupcakes, and showpieces. Modeling chocolate can also be used to enrobe cakes, much like rolled fondant.

Working with Modeling Chocolate

Modeling chocolate is made by adding corn syrup to melted white, milk, or dark chocolate. The result is a solid medium that has the flavor of chocolate but is pliable enough to mold and sculpt. Modeling chocolate's primary use is to create parts of chocolate showpieces or décor that would be difficult to carve or shape out of couverture (such as human faces, flowers, and fruit stems), but it may be used sparingly to create edible dessert containers. Modeling chocolate is also a viable alternative to rolled fondant because it works well for enrobing cakes and is easy to shape into flowers, ropes, ribbons, bows, and other décor elements. White modeling chocolate can also be tinted to any desired color simply by kneading paste food color into it.

Always use a clean rolling pin when rolling out modeling chocolate. When rolling dark or milk modeling chocolate, use cocoa powder to keep it from sticking to the rolling pin and work surface; when rolling white modeling chocolate, use confectioners' sugar. The same modeling tools used for marzipan and sugar pastes also work well with modeling chocolate.

THE BASIC STEPS FOR MODELING A CHOCOLATE ROSE

1. *Each rose will need approximately 4 oz/113 g of modeling chocolate. Knead the modeling chocolate until it is pliable.*

2. *Shape about one-quarter of the modeling chocolate into the center of the rose by shaping it into a cone and then rolling the tip of the cone on the work surface so it is thin. Flatten the bottom of the center so that it stands up on its own.*

3. *Roll out the remaining modeling chocolate on the baking mat until it is ¹⁄₁₆ in/1.5 mm thick.*

4. *Cut out 10 circles with a 1¼-in/3-cm cutter. Remove the excess modeling chocolate and wrap it tightly in plastic warp. Cover the circles with plastic wrap.*

5. *Two of the rounds will be used to make the bud. Attach the first round by connecting it to the tip of the base and then wrapping it around. Smooth the base of this petal into the center of the flower. Repeat this process with the second round. For a more realistic appearance, tuck each petal inside the previous one so they overlap slightly.*

6. *The next row needs three petals that are attached to the bud and slightly overlap. Curl back the edge of one side of each petal and attach the petals so the uncurled side is tucked into the previous petal.*

7. *You can repeat this process with another row of five petals.*

(Please note that the same technique can be applied to making roses out of marzipan and gum paste, if desired. Alternate methods for making gum paste flowers and marzipan flowers are listed on pages 126 and 127).

THE BASIC STEPS FOR MODELING CHOCOLATE LEAVES

1. *Knead a small amount of modeling chocolate until it is pliable.*

2. *Roll out the modeling chocolate on a silicone baking mat until it is ⅛ in/3 mm thick. Cut out leaves with a leaf cutter. Gather the excess modeling chocolate and wrap it tightly in plastic wrap so it does not dry out. Cover the leaf cutouts with a piece of plastic wrap.*

3. *Dust the leaf veiner with cocoa powder if you are using dark or milk modeling chocolate, or cornstarch if you are using white modeling chocolate.*

4. *Vein each leaf and store on a parchment paper–lined sheet pan.*

5. *Once they are dry, brush off any excess cornstarch or cocoa powder.*

(Notes: If you do not have a leaf veiner, you can shape the leaves by draping them over an egg carton. This will bend and shape them to look more realistic. This method may be used for gum paste as well.)

Working with Sugar Pastes

Pastillage is a pure white sugar paste. It is not sensitive to ambient humidity, making it possible to assemble pieces well in advance and hold them at room temperature. Pastillage should not be refrigerated. Gum paste and pastillage are essentially the same medium; however, gum paste is more elastic and may be rolled thinner and manipulated more easily without cracking. Both gum paste and pastillage décor elements should be dried overnight before use.

Since the white paste accentuates any impurities, the work surface and all tools must be kept clean and free of any debris whenever working with sugar pastes. Also, keep sugar paste covered with plastic wrap as much as possible as you work because it dries out very quickly.

Rolled fondant is technically a sugar paste; however, it does not dry to a brittle state as easily and, therefore, cannot be used for the same applications as pastillage or gum paste.

THE BASIC STEPS FOR MAKING A GUM PASTE ROSE

1. *Roll a piece of gum paste with a small rolling pin to ¹⁄₁₆ in/1.5 mm or thinner. Keep the gum paste covered with a piece of plastic wrap when you are not working with it. Have ready a prepared cotton cone with a piece of wire attached to the flat end for the center of the flower.*

2. *Cut a set of petals out of gum paste with a five-petal cutter. Cut the petals apart into one group of two petals and one of three petals. Roll the large end of a gum paste ball tool over the edges of the two-petal group to thin them. With a toothpick or a thin knitting needle, roll up one side of each petal. Roll the toothpick firmly across the surface of the petal to draw up and curl the edge of the petal.*

3. *Turn the petals over and brush the base with gum glue. Without separating the petals, wrap the first petal around the cotton inner cone. The uncurled side of the petal should be wrapped around the cone and the curled side of the petal should be slightly open. Fit the uncurled side of the second petal into the open side of the first petal and wrap the second petal around the first. Press gently to attach the petals to each other and to the cotton cone; the top of the petals should form a tight spiral. (To make a rosebud, follow the procedure to this point, but do not add any more petals.)*

4. *Thin the edges, curl, and brush glue on the three-petal group in the same fashion. Wrap these petals around the first two, overlapping the petals and fitting the third petal inside the uncurled edge of the first. Press gently to attach the petals to one another.*

5. *For a larger rose, cut another group of five petals. Separate them again into one group of two petals and one of three petals. Thin the edges of the two-petal group as above and curl back both edges of each petal. Turn the petals over and brush the base with gum glue. Wrap the petals around the rose as before, overlapping them slightly.*

6. *Thin the edges, curl, and brush glue on the three-petal group in the same fashion. Wrap these petals around the rose, overlapping them. The last petal should overlap the first one of the two-petal group.*

7. *Form a hook out of the end of the wire attached to the inner cotton cone and hang the rose upside down to dry.*

Working with Marzipan

Marzipan is a paste made of ground almonds and sugar. The best-quality marzipan, made with fresh nuts and the proper proportion of sugar, has a fresh, natural flavor. Marzipan can be used as a center (to be enrobed in chocolate), as a confection by itself, or to make décor.

There are a number of methods for making marzipan, but for the small-scale confectioner, the classic French method is the most practical. The nuts are coarsely ground, and a syrup of sugar, water, and glucose is boiled to the appropriate temperature. The cooked syrup is poured over the nuts and they are spread on a lightly oiled marble surface to cool. Once cooled, the sugar-coated nuts are ground to a paste consistency.

The ratio of almonds to sugar varies depending on the intended use of the finished product, as does the temperature to which the syrup is cooked—the hotter the syrup, the firmer the marzipan. For confectionery work, the syrup is usually cooked to 257°F/125°C to make a firm marzipan. The syrup for a pâtisserie marzipan, which is used for fine décor work, is cooked only to 246°F/119°C, resulting in a softer marzipan. Marzipan should be ground in a *mélangeur*, a special machine with adjustable marble rollers. The *mélangeur* produces the smoothest possible finished product. However, if a *mélangeur* is unavailable, a food processor is acceptable.

When marzipan is ground without sufficient moisture, it will separate and appear oily. If this occurs, add a small amount of liquid, either a spirit or syrup, to the marzipan to return it to the proper consistency. The liquid enables the marzipan to re-absorb the oil that has separated out. It may also be necessary to add a small amount of confectioners' sugar.

Marzipan should be firm but not dry or brittle. To fix marzipan that is too hard or dry, massage in a few drops of liquor or glucose. To fix marzipan that is too brittle, for each 2 lb 4 oz/1.25 kg of marzipan, massage in a piece of fondant approximately the size of a walnut. If the marzipan is so soft that it sticks to your hands or the work surface, massage in confectioners' sugar or a mixture of equal parts powdered milk and cornstarch. You can replace from 25 to 50 percent of the almonds in marzipan with other nuts such as hazelnuts or pistachios.

THE BASIC STEPS FOR MAKING MARZIPAN FLOWER CUTOUTS

1. *On a surface dusted with confectioners' sugar, roll a piece of marzipan with a small rolling pin to between 1⁄16 and 1⁄8 in/1.5 and 3 mm thick.*

2. *With a small flower cutter, cut out flower shapes from the marzipan. With the small end of a marzipan ball tool, press the center of each flower into a piece of urethane foam to create an indentation in the center of the flower.*

3. *To make centers for the flowers, shape small pieces of marzipan into tiny balls and place one in the indentation in each flower. Position the centers while the marzipan is still soft so that they will stay in place.*

4. *To create layered flowers, cut flower shapes with different sizes of cutters and different colors of marzipan. Stack the shapes and press them into the foam at the same time.*

THE BASIC STEPS FOR MAKING A MARZIPAN ROSE

1. *Form a small piece of marzipan into a cylinder about 1 1⁄2 in/4 cm long and 1⁄2 in/1 cm in diameter. Make an indentation in the cylinder approximately two-thirds of the way down the cylinder. Taper the top of the cylinder to a point. Stand this cone on your work surface, pressing gently so that the bottom adheres to the surface.*

2. *Form a piece of marzipan into a rope approximately 1⁄2 in/1 cm in diameter and at least 2 in.5 cm long. Cut it into four pieces and roll them into small balls about 1⁄2 in/1 cm in diameter.*

3. *Place the balls on a marble surface, about 2 in/5 cm away from the front edge of the marble. Using a plastic bowl scraper, flatten the front edge of each ball with three short strokes. Use a smooth motion, pushing down on the marzipan and pulling the scraper toward you in one motion. The front edge of the marzipan petals should be very thin but the back edge should remain quite thick. (The difference in thickness will allow you to form a delicate-looking rose that will still support its own weight.)*

4. Holding the blade of a clean, sharp slicer flat against the marble, cut each petal off the marble. Make a small cut in the center of the thick edge of each petal, then overlap the resulting two sections and press them together to form a cupped shape.

5. To form the first inner petal of the flower, place one petal on the prepared marzipan cone, with the thin edge at the top and the thick edge at the indentation in the cone. Hold the petal tightly against the cone and wrap it all the way around the cone so that the edges overlap. The highest point of the petal should be just above the tip of the cone. There should be a tiny hole at the top of the wrapped petal, but the cone should no longer be visible. Use your fingers to gently turn back a small section of the top edge of the petal. Gently squeeze the bottom of the petal into the indentation in the cone.

6. Use the remaining three petals to form the first layer of rose petals: Place one of these petals on the rose, with its center in line with the edge of the first petal. The top of this petal and the subsequent ones should be even with or just slightly above the top of the inner petal. Press the bottom left side of the petal into the rose, leaving the right side open.

7. Position the other two petals in the same fashion, so that their centers line up with the previous petal's left edge, and gently curl the thin right edge of each petal back with your finger. The third petal's left edge should nestle inside the first petal's open right side. Gently press all the petals' bottom edges together and squeeze the bottom of the rose into the indentation in the cone, forming a rounded bottom to the rose.

8. Make another slightly thicker snake out of marzipan and cut it into five pieces. Form these into balls and then petals in the same fashion as above.

9. Use these five petals to form the second layer of rose petals. Place them on the rose in the same fashion, but with each petal overlapping the previous one by only about one-third. The tops of these petals should also be even with or just slightly above those of the previous petals. Gently curl each side of these five petals back and create a crease or point in the middle of the petal.

10. If desired, add another layer of seven petals to the rose.

11. Gently squeeze the bottom of the rose to create a rounded base. Cut the extra marzipan away from the base. Allow the rose to dry at room temperature.

THE BASIC STEPS FOR MAKING MARZIPAN PLAQUES

1. Dust a work surface with confectioners' sugar. Roll a piece of marzipan to $\frac{1}{16}$ in/1.5 mm thick using a small rolling pin.

2. Using a cutter or a template and sharp paring knife, cut a circle, oval, or other desired shape out of the marzipan.

3. Lay the plaque on a flat surface and, using your fingers and the palm of your hand, buff and smooth the cut edges and the top surface of the plaque, being careful not to crack or break the marzipan.

4. Place the plaque on a parchment paper–lined sheet pan and allow to dry at room temperature until it is completely hard. Use an emery board or very fine sandpaper to smooth any rough edges. Pipe lettering on the plaque or decorate as desired.

(Please note that these techniques can also be used to make pastillage flowers and plaques.)

TOOLS FOR CHOCOLATE, CONFECTIONERY, AND DÉCOR

A pastry chef may employ a variety of techniques and materials to craft a look that not only displays creativity and skill but also sets his or her chocolates, confections, cakes, and other desserts apart, and that type of intricate work requires specialized tools.

Piping Tools

Piping tools are invaluable to the pastry chef in order to produce baked goods such as éclairs and macarons as well as delicate icing patterns and royal icing string work. Keep a variety of tips and piping bags on hand in order to meet the needs of the pastry shop.

PIPING BAGS

Piping bags are available in various sizes and can be used to pipe loose-batter cookies and biscuits, truffles, and confections, as well as icings and fillings. Many bakeshops and pastry kitchens have turned to disposable bags to prevent cross contamination and food-borne illness. Reusable bags, which are usually made of nylon or plastic-coated fabric, must be washed with plenty of hot water and enough soap to thoroughly degrease them. Rinse them well and air-dry completely before using again or storing.

Parchment paper cones are an alternative to reusable piping bags. Parchment paper can be purchased precut for rolling into cones, or pastry chefs may cut their own from sheets of parchment paper. The size of the cone depends on the size of the parchment paper triangle. Cones may be rolled, leaving the desired size of opening for piping, or the opening may be cut with scissors after the cone is tightly rolled. Different sizes and shapes of openings may be cut to yield a wide range of décor.

THE BASIC STEPS FOR MAKING PARCHMENT PAPER CONES

1. *Cut a piece of parchment paper 16 by 24 in/41 by 61 cm.*

2. *Place the parchment paper sheet on a flat surface with the length running parallel to the edge of the work surface. Take the lower left-hand corner and bring it up so that the point of the corner is adjacent to and level with the upper right-hand corner; it should look like two peaks of identical height. Firmly crease the fold.*

3. *Insert a long, sharp knife (preferably not serrated) into the folded paper with the edge of the blade toward the creased edge and carefully cut the paper in half at the crease, using a single smooth stroke. The cut edge of each will form the point of each piping cone, so it must be sharp and exact.*

4. *Make a pivot point along the longest edge (opposite the 90-degree angle) of one of the pieces of parchment paper.*

5. *Roll the parchment paper into a funnel shape, making a fine point and folding over the paper to fix the cone in place.*

6. *After filling, crimp and fold over the top edge of the cone.*

LEFT TO RIGHT: Plastic couplers (below), various piping tips (above), parchment paper piping cone, fabric piping bag, plastic piping bag.

Piping Tips

Piping tips, made of nickel-plated metal, are excellent for decorating cakes. They can be used to pipe elaborate borders, shells, pearls, roses and rosettes, lace, and flowers. Commonly piped mediums include royal icing, buttercream, and chocolate.

Piping tips are frequently sold in sets and have numeral identification codes printed on them. The numbers sometimes refer to the diameter of the piping tip and the series. Piping tips can have straight tips, star tips, and any other manner of design.

A plastic coupler is a helpful tool when using piping tips because it allows the user to easily change tips without having to change piping bags. The bottom piece of the coupler goes inside the piping bag first. Then, the piping tip is placed on it and screwed in place with the top piece of the coupler.

A star piping tip can be used to create a number of decorative borders using buttercream icing.

Royal Icing

MAKES 1 LB 3 OZ/539 G

INGREDIENT	U.S.	METRIC
Egg whites	2½ to 3 oz	71 to 85 g
Cream of tartar	¼ tsp	1.25 mL
Confectioners' sugar	1 lb	454 g

1. Place the egg whites in a clean, grease-free mixer bowl. Mix on low speed with the whisk attachment just until the whites begin to break up.

2. Add the cream of tartar and continue mixing on low speed until the whites become frothy.

3. Gradually add the sugar and continue to mix until the icing holds a peak and is dull in appearance.

4. Transfer to a glass container and press a moist towel directly on the surface of the icing. Store under refrigeration, covered tightly with plastic wrap.

NOTES: *If the icing becomes runny, it can be rewhipped each day before use. Sugar or egg whites can be added to adjust the consistency as necessary.*

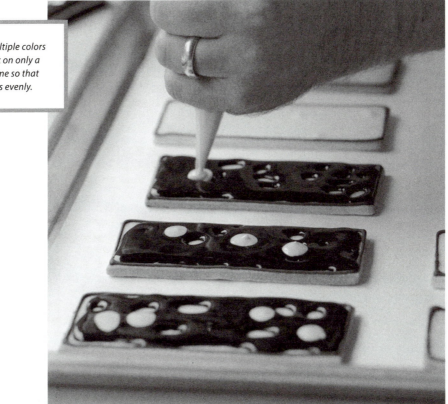

When flooding multiple colors of royal icing, work on only a few cookies at a time so that the royal icing dries evenly.

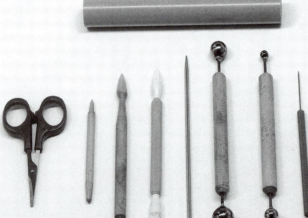

Modeling Tools

There are a variety of modeling tools available today to help make items of marzipan, modeling chocolate, and gum paste look more realistic:

- *veining tools*
- *shell tool*
- *dog bone tool*
- *serrated quilting wheel*
- *cutting wheel*
- *umbrella tool*
- *scribe tool*
- *angler tools*
- *scribe*
- *large and small ball tools*
- *leaf press*
- *needle tool*
- *scissors*

Other modeling tools are used specifically for producing gum paste flowers. These include:

- *plastic work mat*
- *foam flower mat*
- *hard plastic flower mat*

Airbrush

An airbrush is an excellent tool for decorating cakes and pastries in a quick, easy fashion. The ensemble requires a small air compressor, gun, small or large cup, a hose, and liquid food coloring. Airbrushing color onto a cake or cookie allows the baker to quickly color the item as well as use stencils or blend colors flawlessly.

Acetate

Acetate is one of the oldest plastics in use today. As a baking application, acetate sheets can be utilized in several ways. Typically, the sheets are used to create chocolate décor and cutouts, wraparound pieces for cakes and individual desserts, and confections. The acetate adds more shine to chocolate and provides the opportunity to move chocolates for storage while they are setting up. Acetate sheets can be painted with cocoa butter and can be used to transfer designs onto chocolates. Also, acetate sheets are used when making refrigerated desserts, cakes, and pastries.

Heat Gun

A heat gun emits hot air for the purpose of setting or drying items. Its shape is similar to a hair dryer, but the air gets much hotter. The heat gun is useful in bonding luster dust food coloring and for fast melting of small items.

Heating Lamp

A sugar heating lamp is used to keep sugar warm and pliable while pulling and shaping for showpieces. Bulbs for heating lamps range in wattage and are usually made of ceramic. Adjust the height of the bulb to keep the sugar warmer or cooler.

Air Blower

A cool-air blow dryer is used in sugar pulling to cool the sugar down quickly into the desired shape. The cool air helps the sugar keep its shine as well and sets the shape faster.

Sugar Blowing Pump

A blown sugar pump is a handheld device that is used to aerate pulled sugar. Warmed sugar is attached at the end and air is gently pumped by hand through a hose and metal rod into the sugar. Canned gel chafing fuel can be used to help keep the sugar warm. Many shapes can be created, from bubbles to swans. The concept is very similar to blown glass.

CLOCKWISE FROM LEFT: Air blower, sugar pulling tent with heat lamp, canned gel chafing fuel, sugar pump, leaf press, wood-framed warming surface.

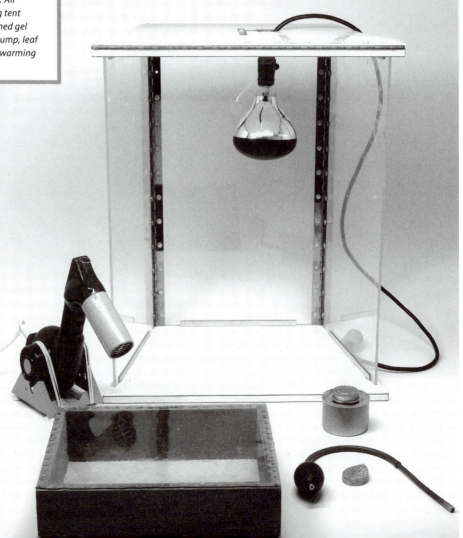

Sugar Pulling Tent

It is important to have an area set up specifically for pulling sugar such as a sugar pulling tent. Sugar pulling tents can be bought commercially or fashioned together on your own. A sugar heat lamp is needed to keep the sugar warm, as well as a wooden warming surface on which to place the sugar. This can be an electrical unit or a simple durable plastic stretched over a wooden frame.

CLOCKWISE FROM BOTTOM:
Caramel bars, copper pot,
fondant funnel.

Fondant Funnel

A fondant funnel is a conical one-handed tool that is used to control the flow of liquids. The hinged handle makes operating rapid and precise, and takes the mess out of glazing and covering pastries. Fondant funnels are typically made of stainless steel and cast aluminum. Different tip sizes are available as are stands to hold the funnel when not in use.

Fondant funnels are used for filling chocolate and molds, glazing cakes, and dispensing sauces. They make covering small items like petits fours and individual desserts fast, easy, and flawless.

Chocolate Tempering Machine

Tempering machines are commonly found in confectionery shops that produce a large volume of chocolate products. These computer controlled machines are made in a wide variety of sizes, and they keep the given amount of chocolate in temper by appropriately heating and cooling the chocolate while continuously agitating it.

Chocolate Spatula

A chocolate spatula, shaped like a bench knife with a handle, is useful for spreading and smoothing chocolate while tempering. It can also be used to make chocolate curls or to wipe chocolate molds after use.

Decorative Transfer Sheets

Transfer sheets are acetate sheets with designs imprinted on them in plain or colored cocoa butter. They are used to imprint designs on chocolate. You can also make your own transfer sheets by painting colored cocoa butter onto plain acetate sheets.

Patterned Rolling Pins

Marzipan and basket-weave rolling pins have a patterned surface to create impressions on marzipan, pastillage, fondant, or gum paste to be used for décor. These pins are made as rod-and-bearing pins or simply as plain cylinders made of nylon or plastic.

Springerle rolling pins are made of wood or plastic resin. They have ornate and intricate pictures or designs in relief that are traditionally used to imprint springerle or gingerbread cookie doughs before baking. Springerle plaques are also available; the plaque is simply pressed into the rolled dough to imprint it before baking.

Copper Pot

A heavy copper pot with a pour spout is very useful for sugar cooking. These pots are available in 5-in/13-cm (holding 24 fl oz/720 mL), 6¼-in/16-cm (holding 50 fl oz/1.5 L), and 8-in/20-cm (holding 3 qt/2.88 L) diameters. Copper is preferred for sugar cooking because it conducts heat evenly.

Chocolate Molds

Chocolate molds are used for making figures, such as an Easter bunny, and for making filled chocolates. Clear rigid polycarbonate plastic molds are easier to care for and use than vacuum plastic molds or tin chocolate molds. However, vacuum plastic molds are relatively inexpensive. Tin molds may be both more elaborate and more durable, but they must be thoroughly cleaned and dried to prevent rusting.

Dipping Tools

Dipping tools include a variety of hand tools consisting of stainless- or nickel-plated steel prongs or loops fastened onto wooden or plastic handles. They are designed for dipping any nut, fruit, ganache, or candy into a chocolate, syrup, or fondant coating.

Chocolate Cutters

Chocolate cutters are made of strong tinned steel or a fiberglass and plastic composite. They range from ¼ to 1½ in/6 to 4 cm in diameter and up to 1 in/3 cm in height. The cutting edges are very sharp. Cutters are often crafted and include animal, geometric, and floral shapes, and more. They are sold individually or in sets that can include as many as 74 pieces.

Caramel Bars

Caramel bars, also called *confectioners' rulers,* are metal bars used for framing ganache or caramel while it is in "liquid" form so that it sets to a specific thickness and dimensions for cutting into individual pieces. They are made of nickel-plated steel and are available in lengths of 20 or 30 in/51 or 76 cm. The bars weigh 6 lb/2.72 kg each, giving them enough weight to contain the liquid confection, and range in height from ⅜ to ½ in/9 mm to 1 cm.

8

BAKEWARE

Bakeware is produced from the same basic materials that are used to make stovetop pots and pans, but since the heat of the oven is less intense of than that of a burner, it is possible to make bakeware from other materials such as glazed and unglazed earthenware, glass, silicone, and ceramics. While there are many multitaskers among the group, like hotel pans, jelly roll pans, and cake pans, the vastly-differing shapes and sizes of bakeware lend themselves to very specific purposes, whether practical or as a matter of tradition. Springform pans are useful when making delicate items that would otherwise be difficult to unmold, whereas brioche molds create an identifiable and traditional shape. Bakeware comes in many different sizes and can also be made from a variety of materials, such as silicone, aluminum, and cast iron, each with its own distinct advantage. Good quality bakeware can be well-maintained through proper use and gentle handling.

PANS

Because form and function are closely related, it is of utmost importance to choose the most appropriate pan for the specific item you are preparing.

Hotel Pan

Hotel pans are stainless-steel pans that come in a number of standard sizes. These pans have a lip that

allows them to hang on storage shelves or steam tables made specifically to the same measurements. They are deeper than sheet pans, making them well suited for use as a hot water bath for baking custards and other preparations that require one.

Baking/Sheet Pan

Baking pans are standard in any kitchen and typically come in three sizes. A full-size sheet pan measures

MIDDLE: Nonstick square cake pan.
CLOCKWISE FROM LEFT: Hotel pan, glass cake pan, baking sheet (bottom), jelly roll pan (top), silicone cake pan, metal round cake pan, metal round cake ring, nonstick round cake pan, metal rectangular cake pan.

18 by 26 in/46 by 66 cm, a half-size sheet pan measures 13 by 18 in/33 by 46 cm, and a quarter-size sheet pan measures 9½ by 13 in/24 by 33 cm. These pans are made of aluminum and come with or without a nonstick coating. The aluminum resists rusting and allows for even heat distribution while baking. Choose a pan that is at least ¹⁄₁₆ in/1.5 mm thick to prevent buckling in a hot oven.

Baking pans have four sides, preventing items from sliding off. They are ideal for baking sheet and roulade cakes, as well as various pastries and cookies. In the pastry kitchen or bakery, they are used for baking cookies and sheet cakes, among other things. Baking sheets can also be inverted and used to create chocolate décor pieces, such as chocolate cigarettes and fans.

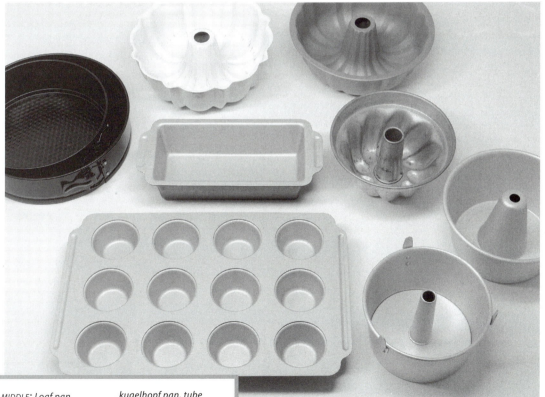

MIDDLE: Loaf pan.
CLOCKWISE FROM LEFT:
Springform pans, Bundt pan, fluted tube pan, kugelhopf pan, tube pan, tube pan with removable bottom, muffin pan.

Jelly Roll Pan

Jelly roll pans are characterized by their 1-in/2.5-cm sides. Coffee cakes, granola bars, and roulades can all be baked in jelly roll pans. Lining the pan with waxed or parchment paper will prevent sticking and make for easy removal; silicone mats are also useful when using jelly roll pans.

Cake Pans

Cake pans are made of various materials, including glass, silicone, tinned steel, and aluminum, with or without a nonstick coating and with or without removable bottoms. They are available in diameters ranging from 2 to 24 in/5 to 61 cm and depths ranging

from 1 to 4 in/3 to 10 cm. Aluminum conducts heat well and thus bakes the most evenly, making it the most common material for cake pans. When using a cake pan, it's best to select one that has sides of at least 2½ in/6 cm and no seams on the inside of the pan.

Springform Pan

Springform pans are used for baking cakes that cannot be inverted to unmold (such as cheesecake and fruit-topped cakes) as well as cakes that have a very delicate structure, making it difficult to unmold them from a traditional, rigid cake pan without damaging them. The ring of a springform pan is joined with a clip closure that creates tension when closed and

CLOCKWISE FROM TOP RIGHT: Ceramic pie pan, aluminum pie pan, glass pie pan, tartlet pans, assorted tart pans, nonstick pie pan.

Vanilla Sponge Cake

MAKES 4 CAKES (8-IN/20-CM DIAMETER EACH)

INGREDIENT	U.S.	METRIC
Butter, melted	9 oz	255 g
Vanilla extract	1 fl oz	30 mL
Eggs	1 lb 11 oz	766 g
Egg yolks	9 oz	255 g
Sugar	1 lb 11 oz	766 g
All-purpose flour, sifted	1 lb 11 oz	766 g

1. Coat the cake pans with a light film of fat and line them with parchment paper circles.

2. Blend the butter with the vanilla.

3. Combine the eggs, egg yolks, and sugar in a mixer bowl. Set over a pan of barely simmering water and whisk constantly until the sugar dissolves and the mixture reaches 110°F/43°C.

4. Transfer to a mixer and whip on high speed with the whisk attachment until the foam reaches maximum volume. Reduce the speed of the mixer to medium and mix for 15 minutes to stabilize the mixture.

5. Fold in the flour. Temper the butter mixture with a small portion of the batter and fold into the larger portion of batter.

6. Scale 1 lb/454 g batter into each prepared cake pan, filling the pans two-thirds full.

7. Bake at 350°F/177°C until the tops of the cakes spring back when lightly touched, about 30 minutes.

8. Cool the cakes in the pans for a few minutes, then unmold onto a sheet pan lined with parchment paper that is dusted with confectioners' sugar to cool completely.

The cake should rise evenly during baking. When it is properly baked, it will just begin to shrink away from the sides of the pan. The surface should spring back when pressed lightly.

holds the removable bottom in place. Springform pans are typically made of aluminum and are available in diameters from 6 to 12 in/15 to 30 cm, with depths ranging from 2½ to 3 in/6 to 8 cm.

TUBE/ANGEL FOOD CAKE PAN

Tube pans have a center tube, so they conduct heat through the center of the batter as well as from the sides and bottom. They are useful for evenly baking heavy batters without overbrowning the outside of the cake. Tube pans also work well for batters that need to bake quickly, such as angel food cake. They are usually made of thin aluminum, with or without a nonstick coating. They come in a range of sizes and may have fluted, molded, or straight sides. A tube pan will normally have three feet on the edge of its rim to facilitate cooling the baked cake.

BUNDT PAN

Bundt pans are shaped much like standard tube pans, but with decoratively fluted edges and a taller center tube. They are made of heavy aluminum with nonstick coating, or of cast iron. Bundt pans are traditionally used for Austrian and German cakes and sweet breads, but have come to be used for a variety of other cakes.

KUGELHOPF/FLUTED TUBE PAN

Traditional German kugelhopf is a yeast dough flavored with raisins, almonds, and cherry brandy. It is baked in a deep tube pan, similar to a Bundt pan, with ornate fluting on the sides. When the cake is unmolded from the pan, it has a pyramid shape. To ensure easy release from the pan, thoroughly butter the pan before filling with dough. Kugelhopf pans are usually made of heavy, tinned steel.

Muffin Pan

Muffin pans are used for baking not only muffins, but also tartlets, cupcakes, and other small cakes. There are three standard sizes: mini (sheets of ten or twelve cups that hold about 1½ tbsp/22.5 mL of batter), regular (sheets of twelve cups that hold about ½ cup/120 mL of batter), and large or jumbo (sheets of six cups that hold about 1 cup/240 mL of batter). Muffin pans may be made of glass, silicone, or aluminum with or without nonstick coating; aluminum conducts heat most evenly, so it makes the best choice for baking muffins.

Tart Pan

Tart pans have fluted sides and removable bottoms. They may be round, square, or rectangular, fluted or straight-sided. They are made of tinned steel, with or without a nonstick coating. They should not have any seams. Round pans range from 4 to 13 in/10 to 33 cm in diameter and ¾ to 2¼ in/2 to 5 cm deep. Square pans are usually 9 in/23 cm across and 1 in/3 cm deep. Rectangular tart pans are 8 by 11 in/20 by 28 cm or 4½ by 14¾ in/11 by 38 cm and 1 in/3 cm deep.

Tartlet pans are most commonly made of tinned steel, with or without a nonstick coating. They come in various shapes and may have removable or fixed bottoms. They range from 1⅛ to 4 in/3 to 10 cm in size (measured across the base). The sides, which may be plain or fluted, are from ½ to ⅝ in/1 to 1.5 cm high.

Pie Pan

Pie pans are round pans with sloping sides, commonly made from glass, earthenware, or metal (with or without nonstick coating). They range from 8 to 10 in/20 to 25 cm in diameter and from 1½ to 3 in/4 to 8 cm deep.

Basic Pie Dough

MAKES 6 LB 6 OZ/2.89 KG

INGREDIENT	U.S.	METRIC
All-purpose flour	3 lb	1.36 kg
Salt	1 oz	28 g
Butter, cut into pieces, chilled	2 lb	907 g
Cold water	16 fl oz	480 mL

1. Combine the flour and salt in the mixer. Add the butter and blend on medium speed with the dough hook attachment until pea-size nuggets form, about 3 minutes. Add the water all at once and continue to mix until the dough just comes together.

2. Turn out the dough onto a lightly floured work surface. Scale the dough as desired. Wrap tightly and refrigerate for at least 1 hour before rolling. (The dough can be held under refrigeration or frozen.)

Pie weights may be used to keep blind-baked tart or pie dough from bubbling up too much during baking.

Rings

CAKE RING

Made of heavy-duty stainless steel, cake rings are bottomless with reinforced straight sides. The rings range in height from 1½ to 3 in/4 to 8 cm, with small to large diameters. Shapes vary as well (round, square, triangular, rectangular, oval, etc.). The sides are welded and polished for a seamless look.

Cake rings are used directly on a baking sheet and can be used to mold frozen desserts, mousse cakes, individual desserts, traditional cakes, and ice cream cakes. The rings make layering easy, and the bottomless design facilitates quick removal. For removal of frozen or mousse cakes, use a blowtorch to gently warm the sides to release the cake. For removal of baked cakes, grease the sides well before baking.

FLAN RING

Flan rings are used for baking and molding tarts and European-style flans. They are made of stainless steel and have rolled edges on both ends. On average, the sides are ¾ in/2 cm high and are available in a variety of diameters. Flan rings can also be used in situations where dough is being used for a shell, like when making a tart. The straight sides of the mold will create distinctive looking tarts. If using a flan ring to make tarts, bake with the ring on top of a sheet pan lined with parchment paper.

Molds

MADELEINE MOLD

A madeleine mold is a tinned steel or aluminum sheet, with or without nonstick coating, with scalloped impressions used for molding the small cakes called madeleines. The impressions come in two standard sizes, large and small, but there may be anywhere from twelve to forty impressions per mold.

BABA MOLD

Baba molds are small, round, straight-sided, bucket-shaped molds used for making babas, the traditional French yeast-raised cakes. It's best to opt for baba molds made of aluminum rather than stainless steel.

STEAMED PUDDING MOLD

Steamed pudding is a dense, chewy cake traditional to Great Britain. A steamed pudding mold is a metal tube with high, decoratively fluted sides with a lid that clamps securely onto the sides to create an airtight seal. The mold is filled with batter and baked in a water bath so that the batter steams inside the mold.

CHARLOTTE MOLD

Shaped like a bucket, charlotte molds are traditionally lined with cake or lady finger cookies before being filled with a mousse or other cream mixture. Charlotte molds are usually made of tinned steel and are available in a variety of sizes.

CLOCKWISE FROM TOP LEFT: Silicone gelatin mold, ceramic shortbread mold, ring molds, springerle pin, madeleine mold, sphere molds, savarin mold, barquette molds, fluted molds, baba mold (left), charlotte mold (right).

Brioche Mold

The classic French shape, *brioche à tête,* is achieved partly with the use of the brioche mold. The sides are fluted and round with sloping edges, and the mold is wider at the top than at the bottom. The flared shape makes for easy release and a distinct look. Brioche molds come in many sizes and are made with tinned steel, featuring nonstick coatings in some versions. If the molds are not nonstick, be sure to butter them before baking and remove the brioche from the mold while they are still slightly warm. In addition to creating buttery, yeasted brioche, the molds can be used to bake shortbreads, tarts, muffins, cakes, sweet loaves, and jellies.

Gelatin Mold

Gelatin molds are traditionally used to shape gelatins, but they can also be used for ice creams, Bavarians, and other mousses. They may be made from tinned steel, anodized aluminum, or copper, and the shape and design can range from simple to highly ornate.

Savarin Mold

Basically shaped like a doughnut, a savarin mold is a round ring mold with a hole in the center. Savarin molds can be made of aluminum, tinned steel, or flexible silicone. These molds are traditionally used for the sweet, rum-soaked French cakes for which they are named, but can also be used to mold other cakes, quick breads, ice creams, mousses, and jellies.

Barquette Mold

Barquettes are boat-shaped tartlet shells that may be filled with any manner of sweet or savory fillings. Barquette molds are available in a variety of sizes and with straight or fluted sides. They are usually made of tinned steel.

Bombe Mold

A bombe mold is a dome-shaped mold used to make mousses and frozen desserts. For easy release, choose bombe molds made of flexible silicone.

LINERS AND MATS

It is often necessary to line a baking pan with a parchment sheet or silicone mat. Some batters and doughs are more likely than others to get stuck to the pan during baking, so the baker must determine which liner is most appropriate for each product. In addition, a cake circle is a special type of liner that is used to give baked cakes support and stability, enabling them to be moved, decorated, and stacked into tiers without crumbling or cracking.

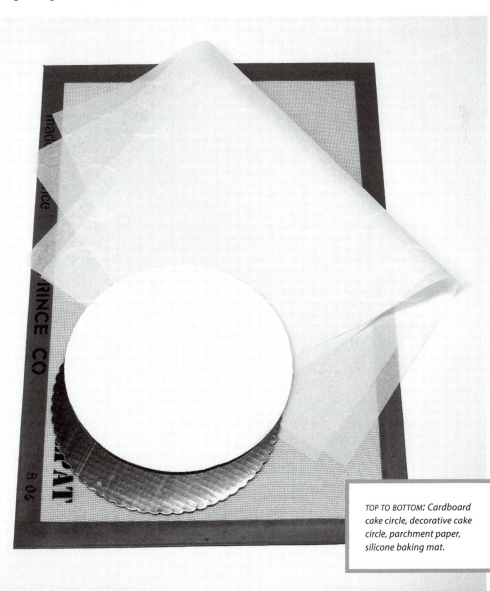

TOP TO BOTTOM: Cardboard cake circle, decorative cake circle, parchment paper, silicone baking mat.

Flexible Silicone Mats

Perhaps the most useful baking equipment technology innovation of the twentieth century, the flexible silicone mat can be used for a wide variety of baking applications. The mat is made of a fiberglass and silicone weave and can be reused thousands of times, making it very environmentally friendly. Silicone mats are effective in temperatures ranging from 40° to 480°F/4° to 249°C and come in a variety of shapes.

The mats never need greasing and provide a nonstick baking surface that can be used on any pan. Baked products are released easily, and the silicone mats produce flatter, rounder cookies due to reduced resistance. The mats also resist liquid, making them effective barriers when needed.

Silicone mats are good for poured sugar, marshmallows, cookies, tuiles, gooey batters, taffy, caramel, and anything sticky in nature. The silicone helps to dissipate heat rapidly in addition to promoting even baking and browning. The cleanup is easy for these mats, with only simple hand washing required to remove all debris.

Parchment Paper

Parchment paper is grease-resistant, nonstick, heat-proof, quick-release coated paper. It has endless uses in the bakeshop and pastry shop, such as lining baking pans and making piping cones for décor work. The paper can be reused until it becomes dark and brittle. It comes in large (full sheet pan size) sheets, in rolls, or precut for special uses such as piping cones or cake pan liners.

Cardboard Cake Circles

Cardboard cakes circles are necessary when decorating and transporting layer cakes. You can cut your own cake circles out of any heavy-duty cardboard, but they are inexpensive to buy premade and are available in a wide range of sizes.

GLOSSARY

ACTIVE DRY YEAST: *A dehydrated form of yeast that needs to be hydrated in warm water (105°F/41°C) before use. It contains about one-tenth the moisture of compressed yeast.*

AERATION: *Incorporation of air by beating or whipping ingredients together.*

ALLOY: *A homogeneous mixture of two or more metals.*

ALPHA CRYSTALS: *Large crystals in untempered chocolate. They are not uniform or stable, and must be melted at 83°F/28°C to properly temper the chocolate.*

AUTOLYSE: *A resting period for dough after mixing the flour and water. This rest allows the dough to fully hydrate and to relax the gluten.*

BAUMÉ (BE): *The scale for expressing the specific gravity of a liquid or the method for measuring the density of sugar syrups. It is expressed in degrees.*

BENCH REST: *In yeast dough production, the stage that allows the gluten in preshaped dough to relax before the final shaping. Also known as secondary fermentation.*

BETA CRYSTALS: *The small, stable fat crystals that give chocolate its shine and snap.*

BIGA: *Italian for an aged dough. A type of pre-ferment containing 50 to 60 percent water.*

BLADE: *The portion of a knife that is used for cutting, slicing, and chopping.*

BOLSTER: *In a knife, the thick band of steel between the body of the blade and the handle. Also referred to as the shank.*

BONING KNIFE: *A knife of varying length and flexibility used primarily in the butchering and fabrication of meat and poultry and sometimes fish.*

BRIX SCALE: *A scale of measurement (decimal system) used to determine the density and concentration of sugar in a solution. It is expressed in degrees.*

CARBON STEEL: *An alloy of carbon and steel used to make knife blades; it takes a good edge and resists discoloration and staining.*

CARBORUNDUM STONE: *A sharpening stone available in various "grits" to sharpen knives to the desired degree of fineness. A man-made abrasive material used in the manufacture of sharpening stones.*

CHEF'S KNIFE: *An all-purpose knife used for chopping, slicing, and mincing. The blade is usually between 8 and 14 inches long. Also referred to as a French knife or cook's knife.*

COUVERTURE: *A type of chocolate specifically designed for coating or incorporation with other ingredients. Extra cocoa butter is added to increase its smoothness, flexibility, and gloss after tempering. The cocoa butter content of couverture should be at least 32 percent.*

CRITICAL CONTROL POINT (CCP): *The points at the appropriate stages in the formula to indicate temperatures and times for safe food-handling procedures during storage, preparation, holding, and reheating.*

CROSS CONTAMINATION: *The transference of disease-causing elements from one source to another through physical contact.*

CRUMB: *The interior texture of baked goods.*

CRYSTALLIZATION: *A process that occurs when sugar is deposited from a solution.*

DIAMOND-IMPREGNATED STEEL OR STONE: *A sharpening or honing tool that has been produced with industrial-grade diamonds over the surface.*

DOCK: *To pierce dough lightly with a fork or dough docker (resembles a spiked paint roller) to allow steam to escape during baking. This helps the dough to remain flat and even.*

DOUGH: *A mixture of ingredients high in stabilizers and often stiff enough to cut into shapes.*

EMULSION: *The suspension of two ingredients that do not usually mix. Butter is an emulsion of water in fat.*

ENRICHED DOUGH: *Dough that is enriched includes ingredients that add fat or vitamins. Examples of these ingredients are sugar, eggs, milk, and fats.*

FERMENTATION: *A process that happens in any dough containing yeast. As the yeast eats the sugars present in the dough, carbon dioxide is released, which causes the dough to expand. It begins as soon as the ingredients are mixed together and continues until the dough reaches an internal temperature of 138°F/59°C during baking. Fermentation alters the flavor and appearance of the final product.*

FOAMING: *The process of beating eggs (whole eggs, yolks, or whites) to incorporate air until they form a light, fluffy substance with many small air bubbles.*

FOLDING: *(1) Incorporating a lighter mixture into a heavier one. (2) The process of bending a dough over itself during the bulk fermentation stage to redistribute the available food supply for the yeast, equalize the temperature of the dough, expel gases, and further develop the gluten in the dough.*

FONDANT: *Sugar, cooked with corn syrup, that is induced to crystallize by constant agitation, in order to produce the finest possible crystalline structure. Fondant is used as centers in chocolate production, and as a glaze in pastries.*

GANACHE: *An emulsion of chocolate and cream. Ganache may also be made with butter or other liquids in place of the cream.*

GELATIN: *A protein derived from the skins and tendons of animals. Gelatin is used as a binder and stabilizer. It is available in granulated and sheet forms.*

GUIDING HAND: *The hand holding the item to be cut and acting as a guide to the knife blade.*

GUM PASTE: *A white modeling substance made from gum tragacanth or gelatin, water, glucose, and sugar.*

HAZARD ANALYSIS OF CRITICAL CONTROL POINTS (HACCP): *A method of preventing food-borne disease by identifying potentially hazardous "control points" in the flow of food products through the production process and designing the process to eliminate contamination.*

HANDLE: *The part of a knife that is held. It may be made of various materials, including wood, plastic, wood impregnated with plastic, rubber-like compounds, and steel.*

HEEL: *The back edge of a knife closest to the handle, used for tough jobs where weight and strength are required, such as cutting hard vegetables, bones, or shells.*

HYDROGENATION: *The process in which hydrogen atoms are added to an unsaturated fat molecule, making it partially or completely saturated at room temperature. Vegetable oils are hydrogenated to create shortening.*

HYDROLYZE: *To chemically split one compound into other compounds by taking up the elements of water. Cornstarch is hydrolyzed to produce corn syrup.*

HYGROSCOPIC: *Having the property of absorbing moisture from the air. Sugar and salt are both hygroscopic ingredients.*

LAMINATION: *The technique of creating alternating layers of fat and dough through a process of repeated rolling and folding.*

LEAN DOUGH: *A yeast dough that does not contain fats or sugar.*

LEAVENING: *Raising or lightening by air, steam, or gas (carbon dioxide). In baking, leavening occurs with yeast (organic), baking powder or baking soda (chemical), and steam (physical/mechanical).*

MISE EN PLACE: *French for "put in place." The preparation and assembly of ingredients, pans, utensils, and plates or serving pieces needed for a particular dish or service period.*

PARING KNIFE: *A small knife with a blade ranging in length from 2 to 4 inches, is used primarily for trimming and peeling vegetables.*

PASTILLAGE: *See Gum Paste.*

PH SCALE: *A scale with values from 0 to 14 representing degrees of acidity. A pH of 7 is neutral, 0 is most acidic, and 14 is most alkaline. Chemically, pH measures the concentration and activity of the element hydrogen.*

PHYSICAL LEAVENING: *A process that occurs when air and/or moisture that is trapped during the mixing process expands as it is heated. This can occur through foaming, creaming, or lamination. Also known as mechanical leavening.*

POOLISH: *A semiliquid starter dough with equal parts (by weight) of flour and water blended with yeast and allowed to ferment for 3 to 15 hours.*

PRE-FERMENT: *A piece of dough saved from the previous day's production to be used in the following day's dough.*

PRESHAPING: *The gentle first shaping of dough. Also known as rounding.*

PROOF: *To allow yeast dough to rise.*

SCALE: *(1) To measure ingredients by weight. (2) To multiply or divide the quantities in a formula to change the yield. (3) To portion batter or dough according to weight or size.*

SCORE: *To make incisions into dough that allow steam to escape and the crust to expand. Also known as slashing or docking.*

SHARPENING STONE: *A stone used to sharpen the edge of a dull knife.*

SLICER, SLICING KNIFE: *A long knife with a relatively narrow blade used principally for carving and slicing larger cuts of cooked, roasted, or smoked items.*

STEEL: *(1) A tool used to maintain knife blades. It is usually made of steel but may be ceramic, glass, or diamond-impregnated metal. Sometimes referred to as a sharpening or honing steel. (2) An alloy of iron with carbon (carbon steel) and perhaps several other metals, including nickel, chromium, and molybdenum, to increase the hardness and/or resilience of the iron.*

STEELING: *To realign, straighten and/or maintain the edge of a knife.*

TEMPER: *(1) To melt, agitate, and cool chocolate to ensure it retains its smooth gloss, crisp "snap" feel, and creamy texture. (2) To heat gently and gradually, as in the process of incorporating hot liquid into a liaison to gradually raise its temperature.*

VISCOSITY: *The quantity that describes a fluid's resistance to flow.*

WHISK: *To beat an item, such as cream or egg whites, to incorporate air.*

APPENDIX

Weight Measure Conversions

U.S.	METRIC
¼ ounce	7 grams
½ ounce	14 grams
1 ounce	28.4 grams
4 ounces	113 grams
8 ounces (½ pound)	227 grams
16 ounces (1 pound)	454 grams
32 ounces (2 pounds)	907 grams
40 ounces (2½ pounds)	1.134 kilograms

Volume Measure Conversions

U.S.	METRIC
1 teaspoon	5 milliliters
1 tablespoon	15 milliliters
1 fluid ounce (2 tablespoons) 30 milliliters	
2 fluid ounces (¼ cup)	60 milliliters
8 fluid ounces (1 cup)	240 milliliters
16 fluid ounces (1 pint)	480 milliliters
32 fluid ounces (1 quart)	960 milliliters (0.95 liter)
128 fluid ounces (1 gallon)	3.84 liters

These measurements are exact. For ease of use in the kitchen, the measurements in the recipes are rounded to the nearest whole number.

Temperature Conversions

DEGREES FAHRENHEIT (°F)	DEGREES CELSIUS (°C)
32°	0°
40°	4°
140°	60°
150°	66°
160°	71°
170°	77°
212°	100°
275°	135°
300°	149°
325°	163°
350°	177°
375°	191°
400°	204°
425°	218°
450°	232°
475°	246°
500°	260°

Celsius temperatures have been rounded.

Information, Hints, and Tips for Calculations

1 gallon = 4 quarts = 8 pints = 16 cups (8 fluid ounces per cup) = 128 fluid ounces
1 fifth bottle = approximately 1½ pints or exactly 25.6 fluid ounces
1 measuring cup holds 8 fluid ounces (a coffee cup generally holds 6 fluid ounces)
1 egg white = 2 fluid ounces (average)
1 lemon = 1 to 1¼ fluid ounces juice
1 orange = 3 to 3¼ fluid ounces juice
To convert ounces and pounds to grams:
Multiply ounces by 28.35 to determine grams; multiply pounds by 453.59 to determine grams
To convert Fahrenheit to Celsius:
Subtract 32 from °F and divide by 1.8 to determine °C
To convert pounds to kilograms:
Divide pounds by 2.2 to determine kilograms
To convert grams to ounces or pounds:
Divide grams by 28.35 to determine ounces; divide grams by 453.59 to determine pounds
To convert fluid ounces to milliliters:
Multiply fluid ounces by 30 to determine milliliters
To convert milliliters to fluid ounces:
Divide milliliters by 30 to determine fluid ounces
Metric prefixes:
kilo = 1,000
hecto = 100
deca = 10
deci = 1/10
centi = 1/100
milli = 1/1000

Converting to Common Unit of Measure

To convert measurements to a common unit (by weight or volume), use the following chart. This information is used both to convert scaled measurements into practical and easy-to-use recipe measures and to determine costs.

Common Unit Conversions

U.S. MEASURE	VOLUME	VOLUME (FLUID OUNCES)
1 pound	16 ounces (weight)	Varies by product
1 gallon	4 quarts	128 fluid ounces
1 quart	2 pints	32 fluid ounces
1 pint	2 cups	16 fluid ounces
1 cup	16 tablespoons	8 fluid ounces
1 tablespoon	3 teaspoons	½ fluid ounce

READINGS AND RESOURCES

Baking and Pastry

Alford, Jeffrey, and Naomi Duguid. *Flatbreads and Flavors: A Baker's Atlas.* New York: HarperCollins, 2008.

Amendola, Joseph, and Nicole Rees. *The Baker's Manual,* 5th ed. Hoboken, NJ: John Wiley & Sons, 2002.

Amendola, Joseph, and Nicole Rees. *Understanding Baking,* 3rd ed. Hoboken, NJ: John Wiley & Sons, 2003.

Beranbaum, Rose Levy. *The Pie and Pastry Bible.* New York: Scribner, 1998.

France, Wilfred J., and Michael R. Small, eds. *The New International Confectioner,* 5th ed. New York: Van Nostrand Reinhold, 1981.

Friberg, Bo. *The Professional Pastry Chef,* 4th ed. Hoboken, NJ: John Wiley & Sons, 2002.

Hensperger, Beth. *The Bread Bible: Beth Hensperger's 300 Favorite Recipes.* San Francisco: Chronicle, 2004.

Malgieri, Nick. *Nick Malgieri's Perfect Pastry.* New York: Macmillan, 1998.

Richemont Craft School. *Swiss Confectionery,* 3rd ed. Lucerne, Switzerland: Richemont Craft School, 1997.

Silverton, Nancy. *Nancy Silverton's Breads from the La Brea Bakery: Recipes for the Connoisseur.* New York: Villard, 1996.

Sultan, William J. *Practical Baking,* 5th ed. New York: John Wiley & Sons, 1996.

Chemistry of Cooking

Charley, Helen, and Connie M. Weaver. *Foods: A Scientific Approach,* 3rd ed. Saddle River, NJ: Prentice-Hall, 1997.

Corriher, Shirley. *CookWise: The Secrets of Cooking Revealed.* New York: Morrow/Avon, 1997.

Griswold, Ruth M., and Ada Marie Campbell, and Marjorie Porter Penfield. *The Experimental Study of Food,* 2nd ed. Boston: Houghton Mifflin, 1979.

McGee, Harold. *The Curious Cook: More Kitchen Science and Lore.* New York: Hungry Minds, 1992.

McGee, Harold. *On Food and Cooking: The Science and Lore of the Kitchen.* New York: Scribner, 2004.

Equipment and Mise en Place

Aronson, Emily, and Florence Fabricant, and Burt Wolf. *The New Cook's Catalogue: The Definitive Guide to Cooking Equipment.* New York: Knopf, 2000.

The Culinary Institute of America. *The Professional Chef's Knife Kit,* 2nd ed. New York: John Wiley & Sons, 1999.

Schmidt, Arno. *The Chef's Book of Formulas, Yields and Sizes,* 3rd ed. Hoboken, NJ: John Wiley & Sons, 2003.

Scriven, Carl, and James Stevens. *Food Equipment Facts: A Handbook for the Foodservice Industry,* 2nd ed. New York: John Wiley & Sons, 1989.

Williams, Chuck. The Williams-Sonoma Cookbook and Guide to Kitchenware. New York: Random House, 1986.

Dictionaries and Encyclopedias

Bickel, Walter. *Herings Dictionary of Classical and Modern Cookery.* New York: French and European Publications, 1981.

Cost, Bruce. *Asian Ingredients: A Guide to the Foodstuffs of China, Japan, Korea, Thailand, and Vietnam.* New York: HarperCollins, 2000.

Coyle, Patrick L. *The World Encyclopedia of Food.* New York: Facts on File, 1982.

Davidson, Alan. *The Oxford Companion to Food.* New York: Oxford University Press, 1999.

Del Conte, Anna. *Gastronomy of Italy.* Upper Saddle River, NJ: Prentice-Hall, 1988.

Dowell, Philip, and Adrian Bailey. *The Cook's Ingredients.* Pleasantville, NY: Reader's Digest Association, 1990.

Herbst, Sharon. *Food Lover's Companion,* 4th ed. Hauppage, NY: Barron's, 2001.

Jacobs, Jay. *Gastronomy.* New York: Newsweek Books, 1975.

Knight, John B., and Charles A. Salter, eds. *Knight's Foodservice Dictionary.* New York: John Wiley & Sons, 1987.

Lang, Jenifer Harvey, ed. *Larousse Gastronomique.* New York: Crown, 1988.

Maree, Aaron. *Patisserie: An Encyclopedia of Cakes, Pastries, Cookies, Biscuits, Chocolate, Confectionery and Desserts.* New York: HarperCollins, 1994.

Mariani, John F. *The Encyclopedia of American Food and Drink.* New York: Lebhar-Friedman, 1999.

Passmore, Jacki. *The Encyclopedia of Asian Food and Cooking.* New York: Hearst, 1991.

Raymond Oliver. *Gastronomy of France.* Translated by Claud Durrell. New York: Wine & Food Society with World Publishing, 1967.

Riely, Elizabeth. *The Chef's Companion: A Concise Dictionary of Culinary Terms,* 2nd ed. New York: John Wiley & Sons, 1996.

Rubash, Joyce. *The Master Dictionary of Food and Wine,* 2nd ed. New York: John Wiley & Sons, 1996.

Simon, André Louis. *A Concise Encyclopedia of Gastronomy.* New York: Overlook, 1983.

Von Welanetz, Diana, and Paul von Welanetz. The Von Welanetz Guide to Ethnic Ingredients. New York: Warner, 1987.

General and Classical Cookery

Bennion, Marion. *Introductory Foods,* 11th ed. Upper Saddle River, NJ: Prentice-Hall, 1999.

Bocuse, Paul. *Paul Bocuse's French Cooking.* Translated by Colette Rossant. New York: Pantheon, 1987.

Brillat-Savarin, Jean-Anthelme. *The Physiology of Taste, or Meditations on Transcendental Gastronomy.* Washington, D.C.: Counterpoint, 2000.

The Culinary Institute of America. *The Professional Chef,* 8th ed. Hoboken, NJ: John Wiley & Sons, 2006.

Dornenberg, Andrew, and Karen Page. *Culinary Artistry.* New York: John Wiley & Sons, 1991.

Escoffier, Auguste. *The Complete Guide to the Art of Modern Cookery.* New York: John Wiley & Sons, 1995.

Escoffier, Auguste. *Escoffier Cook Book.* New York: Crown, 1941.

Escoffier, Auguste. *Le Guide Culinaire: The Complete Guide to the Art of Modern Cookery.* Translated by H. L. Cracknell and R. J. Kaufmann. New York: John Wiley & Sons, 1979.

Fuller, John, and Edward Renold, and David Faskett. *The Chef's Compendium of Professional Recipes,* 3rd ed. London: Butterworth-Heinemann, 1992.

Gielisse, Victor. *Cuisine Actuelle.* Boulder, CO: Taylor Publications, 1992.

Metz, Ferdinand E., and the U.S. Team. *Culinary Olympics Cookbook: U.S. Team Recipes from the International Culinary Olympics.* Edited by Steve M. Weiss. Silver Spring, MD: Cahners, 1983.

Millau, Christian. *Dining in France.* New York: Stewart, Tabori & Chang, 1986.

Pauli, Eugene. *Classical Cooking the Modern Way,* 3rd ed. New York: John Wiley & Sons, 1999.

Pépin, Jacques. *La Technique.* New York: Simon & Schuster, 1989.

Peterson, James. *Essentials of Cooking.* New York: Artisan, 2000.

Point, Ferdinand. *Ma Gastronomie.* Translated by Frank Kulla and Patricia S. Kulla. Chicago: Lyceum, 1974.

Saulnier, Louis. *Le Répertoire de la Cuisine.* Hauppage, NY: Barron's, 1977.

Wolfe, Kenneth C. *Cooking for the Professional Chef.* Clifton Park, NY: Delmar, 1982.

INDEX

Page numbers in *italics* indicate illustrations